OPERA
SMALL
TALK

pocket plots

crucial characters

amusing asides

ILLUSTRATIONS BY ANNETTE CATE

Copyright © 1993 by Robert Levine and
Elizabeth Lutyens

Published by Cherubino Press
Box 615, Concord MA 01742

Illustrations by Annette Cate
Design by Sally Reed
Type by Quick Brown Fox, Groton MA

Library of Congress Cataloging-in-Publication Data

Levine, Robert and Lutyens, Elizabeth
    Opera Small Talk:
    Pocket Plots, Crucial Characters, Amusing Asides

Operas--casts, plot summaries, background information
and anecdotes. Illustrations.

ISBN 0-9638743-0-6
Library of Congress Catalog Card Number 93-80148

PRINTED IN THE UNITED STATES OF AMERICA

Contents

GIUSEPPE VERDI

Aida

Four Acts: First Performance—Cairo
(Opera House), 1871
Libretto by A. Ghislanzoni, C. du Locle

WHERE AND WHEN
Egypt, time of the Pharaohs

WHO'S WHO
Aida, the Ethiopian princess (soprano)
Amneris, the Egyptian princess to whom Aida is enslaved
(mezzo-soprano)
Radames, Egyptian soldier, lover of Aida (tenor)
Amonasro, King of Ethiopia, Aida's father (baritone)

WHAT IT'S ABOUT
Aida faces a familiar princess problem: should she be loyal
to her people—or to the man she loves? Her decision will
determine the destinies of two warring nations as well as
the individual fates of those in charge. Dilemma makes
powerful tension, and herein lies the tale.

WHAT'S HAPPENING
Act I opens with news that Ethiopian forces are approach-
ing the Valley of the Nile. Radames takes command of the
Egyptian troops, and Aida wishes she could cheer simulta-
neously for her lover and her homeland. Amneris ushers in
Act II with preparations for honors due the triumphant
Radames. She wants him for her own, even when she discovers he has eyes only for her slave. As Radames enters
the victor's circle, he longs to ask for Aida's hand in marriage; instead, he gets Amneris. Act III opens on a secluded
bank of the Nile where Aida waits to discuss this awful
turn of events with Radames. Her father appears in disguise, and convinces her that the only way she can be united with her lover, her home, and her family is to trick
Radames into betraying his army. She succeeds, and
Amneris overhears everything. Radames is arrested as Aida
and her father flee. In the final Act, Amneris overcomes

her jealousy and offers to rescue Radames. He refuses, choosing live burial over life without Aida. However, Aida will be his after all: she is waiting for him, concealed behind the altar of the tomb.

WHAT'S MORE. . .

When the Khedive of Egypt invited Verdi to compose a grand opera for Cairo's Opera House, the composer was not interested. However, he caved in when he saw an accompanying letter suggesting that if he, Verdi, were not interested, then "Wagner might do something really good." After delays, *Aida* was unveiled, and the production was more than lavish: Radames' shield and helmet were cast of solid silver, and more than 300 people were on stage. The audience was a who's who of European and Egyptian society, and the Khedive's harem alone took up three loges! Verdi stayed away, writing that the occasion made him feel "disgust and humiliation," and that his opera had become "no longer art . . . [but] a pleasure party, a hunt." However, the success of *Aida*—then, as now—is due as much to its inherent musical value as to the production values which can be placed upon it: Verdi never sold out.

WHAT TO LISTEN FOR

Act I: Radames' aria "Celeste Aida," which is a poem to his beloved; Aida's "Ritorna vincitor," where she tries to reconcile her feelings for her lover and her country.
Act II: The Triumphal Scene, in which all characters voice their conflicting emotions.
Act III: Aida's "O patria mia," and Act IV: Amneris's Judgment Scene.

UMBERTO GIORDANO

Andrea Chénier

Four Acts: First Performance—Milan (La Scala),
1896   Libretto by Luigi Illica

WHERE AND WHEN
Paris in the time of the French Revolution

WHO'S WHO
Andrea Chénier, a poet (tenor)
Maddalena de Coigny, wealthy aristocrat (soprano)
Carlo Gérard, a de Coigny servant; later, a Revolutionary
(baritone)

WHAT IT'S ABOUT

There was a real André Chénier,
who, like the fictional one,
was a poet and philoso-
pher; however, the real
man was also a
Revolutionary. The
operatic Chénier
tries to remain
outside the
events of

the time, focusing instead on romantic love and on faith in a "sovereign power." Fact and fiction do converge at the end, as the character, like the real man, falls victim to the Revolution.

WHAT'S HAPPENING

In Act I, at a soirée given by the Countess de Coigny, Chénier recites for Maddalena, whom he loves, decrying man's misery in contrast to nature's beauty. Gérard, who secretly desires Maddalena, bursts into the party leading a band of beggars, but the guests are unaware of the danger this heralds. Act II brings the Revolution in full swing, with Gérard as one of its leaders. Chénier and Maddalena reunite, but he is wanted as a counter-revolutionary. A spy tracks him down, but Gérard warns him in time. In Act III, Gérard's love for Maddalena has been rekindled, and his patriotic zeal and jealousy combine to make him sign the indictment against Chénier. Maddalena offers herself to Gérard, who then admits the charges were false, but they are both too late. Act IV. At the prison: Maddalena changes places with a condemned woman; she goes with Chénier to the guillotine.

WHAT'S MORE . . .

In 1888, music publisher Edoardo Sanzogno created a competition for composers of one-act operas. As history knows, Mascagni's *Cavalleria Rusticana* was the winner, but Umberto Giordano, another entrant, showed enough promise for Sanzogno to commission another work from him. Giordano's subsequent two tries were flops, but Sanzogno stuck by him anyway. *Andrea Chénier* was the next opera, and when Sanzogno's advisors told him that "it was not worth a fig," Mascagni intervened, convincing Sanzogno of its stageworthiness. And it was, in fact, a resounding success—there were 20 curtain calls for singers and Giordano—and the tenor, particularly, was applauded—as tenors have been in the title role since then. *Chénier's* theatricality always wins the audience over, not to mention its tunefulness: "You have only to find a beautiful melody and build an opera around it," said Giordano, and he seems to have been right.

WHAT TO LISTEN FOR

Act I: Chénier's "Improvviso" - "Un di all'azzurro spazio." Act II: Chénier-Maddalena duet "Ecco l'altare . . . Eravate possente, Ora soave." Act III: Gérard's aria "Nemico della patria"; Maddalena's aria "La mamma morta." Act IV: Chénier's aria "Come un bel di di Maggio"; final duet "Vicino a te."

GIUSEPPE VERDI

Un ballo in maschera
(A Masked Ball)

Three Acts: First Performance—Rome
(Teatro Apollo) 1859
Libretto by Antonio Somma

WHERE AND WHEN
Boston, late 17th century

WHO'S WHO
Riccardo, Governor of Boston (tenor) [Gustav III]
Renato, his friend and counsel (baritone) [Anckarstroem]
Amelia, Renato's wife (soprano)
Ulrica, a fortune teller (contralto) [Arvidson]
Oscar, the Governor's page (soprano)

WHAT IT'S ABOUT
This is a multinational opera. The characters have Italian names; the setting is Boston, Massachusetts, USA; and the story is based on a true incident that occurred in Sweden in 1792: the assassination of King Gustav III at the Stockholm Opera House. (See **What's More . . .** opposite page.)

WHAT'S HAPPENING
In Act I, Riccardo is so engrossed in his desire for Amelia that he pays little heed to Renato's warnings of political intrigue. It is also Renato who steps forward when the fortune teller Ulrica predicts that the next man to take Riccardo's hand will be his murderer. Aware that Renato is both loyal and oblivious to the romance between Amelia and himself, Riccardo can only scoff. Amelia, in Act II, tries to exorcise her love for Riccardo with Ulrica's "cure" of herbs she must gather at midnight under the scaffold. Riccardo discovers her there, but they are interrupted by Renato, who has come to offer protection. He does not recognize the heavily-veiled woman as his wife, until conspirators leap out and tear off her disguise. Act III reveals a bitter and vengeful Renato. He joins the conspirators and, at a costume ball, he gets Oscar to point out the mask that

conceals his master's face. Renato kills Riccardo, fulfilling Ulrica's prophecy.

WHAT'S MORE . . .

Regicide portrayed onstage, particularly in nineteenth century Italy? Never! Verdi was forced to try alternatives. He at first wanted *Ballo* presented in the kingdom of Naples, so he reset the opera in Pomerania, with a fictitious Duke at its center. But he arrived in Naples to begin rehearsals on the very day of an assassination attempt against Napoleon. The censors demanded such complete alterations that Verdi withdrew the opera rather than submit. More liberal Rome accepted it set in Boston—a very faraway place to the Italians (what was a governor, anyway?). When Paris presented *Ballo* in 1861, it was set in Florence; and in London, it was set in Naples. Nowadays, with daily news being so horrifying, it is more often than not set where Verdi wanted it—in Stockholm—but it took until 1958 for the first complete, uncensored performance to take place!

WHAT TO LISTEN FOR

Act I: Renato's aria "Alla vita che t'arride"; Ulrica's incantation "Re dell'abissso affrettati"; Riccardo's aria "Di tu se fedele." Act II:
Amelia's aria "Ecco l'orrido campo"; Riccardo-Amelia duet "Teco io sto." Act III: Amelia's aria "Morro, ma prima in grazia"; Renato's aria "Eri tu"; Riccardo's aria "Forse la soglia attinse."

GIOACHINO ROSSINI

Il barbiere di Siviglia

(The Barber of Seville)

Two Acts: First Performance, Rome
(Teatro Argentina)   1816
Libretto by Cesare Sterbini

WHERE AND WHEN
Seville, 17th century

WHO'S WHO
Figaro, a barber (baritone)
Count Almaviva (tenor)
Rosina (mezzo-soprano)
Dr. Bartolo, her guardian (baritone)
Don Basilio, music teacher (bass)

WHAT IT'S ABOUT
Rosina must escape from Dr. Bartolo, who intends to
marry her. With the assistance of her true love (the Count)
and a busybody barber (Figaro), the wealthy—and strong-
willed— young beauty is bound to get her way.

WHAT'S HAPPENING
In Act I, Count Almaviva enlists Figaro's help to win
Rosina's affections. First he serenades her, pretending to be
a poor student named Lindoro. Then, hearing that Bartolo
plans to wed Rosina the very next day, the Count gets
Figaro to help him infiltrate the household disguised as a
drunken soldier. By Act II, the plot has spun itself into
dizzying twists, and the Count makes a fresh appearance,
now disguised as the new music teacher. At first, Rosina is
delighted, recognizing him as Lindoro, but then she learns
he is really the Count; furthermore, thanks to phony evidence rigged by Bartolo and Basilio, she thinks he has been
unfaithful. Furious, she agrees to wed Bartolo, but Figaro
and the Count rush in to set the story straight. The lovers
finagle Bartolo's notary into making them man and wife.

WHAT'S MORE . . .

Opening nights of
opera are always an
event, but *The Barber
of Seville*'s was one in
a million. Rossini,
conducting from
the harpsichord,
was wearing a
jacket which had
been given to him
by the manage-
ment; it was
too small for
his plump
body, and
the audience
immediately
began to laugh.
Then, a guitar
string broke
during the
tenor's on-stage
serenade, and this
brought on more

ridicule. When the Rosina—a local favorite—made her
first, very brief appearance, the audience thought she'd
have little to do and became angry. A bit later, the Don
Basilio tripped and fell, continuing to sing while his nose
bled. And when a cat happened on stage and meowed nois-
ily, there was no chance of regaining decorum. But the real
reason for the fiasco was probably the fact that Paisiello's
Il barbiere di Siviglia had been a great favorite and his fans,
angry because Rossini had usurped the plot, came to dis-
rupt the evening. But the excellence and vivacity of
Rossini's score won—by the second performance all was
well—and has been since.

WHAT TO LISTEN FOR

Act I: Almaviva's serenade "Ecco ridente in cielo"; Figaro's
aria "Largo al factotum"; Rosina's aria "Una voce poco
fa"; Rosina-Figaro duet "Dunque io son"; ensemble
finale "Fredda ed immobile." Act II: Rosina's lesson scene
"Contro un cor"; ensemble "Buona sera, mio signore";
trio "Ah! Qual colpo."

GIACOMO PUCCINI

La bohème

(freely translated *The Bohemian Life*)

Four Acts: First Performance—
Turin (Teatro Regio) 1896
Libretto by Luigi Illica and Giuseppe Giacosa

WHERE AND WHEN
Latin Quarter of Paris and environs; about 1830

WHO'S WHO
Rodolfo, a poet (tenor)
Marcello, a painter (baritone)
Colline, a philosopher (bass)
Schaunard, a musician (baritone)
Mimi, a seamstress (soprano)
Musetta, a singer (soprano)

WHAT IT'S ABOUT
A cold garret room is home to four struggling artists. In spite of the young men's poverty, they radiate camaraderie and *joie de vivre*. However, when romance enters the scene, the simple life takes on complications--and tragedy.

WHAT'S HAPPENING
Act I: Rodolfo meets and falls in love with Mimi, a frail seamstress who lives on the floor below, and, in Act II, Mimi joins the men for Christmas Eve dinner at a café. As she responds to admiring glances, Rodolfo shows the first signs of a jealous lover. Marcello is no stranger to this condition, having spotted his former sweetheart, Musetta, dining nearby. She refocuses her charms on Marcello, and they reunite. By Act III, Mimi's health has worsened—on top of that, Rodolfo's jealousy is tearing them apart. She overhears him tell Marcello that she is a flirt and then go on to confess his real fear: that Mimi is dying and beyond his help. Shocked, she sees that she and her poet must part. After an argument, Musetta and Marcello make the same decision. Back in the garret in Act IV, the artist friends mask their troubles with jokes and high jinks. Musetta suddenly appears, bringing Mimi for her final farewell.

When she dies, Rodolfo will not believe it until he sees the pain on the others' faces. Then he can only cry out "Mimi! Mimi!" as the curtain falls.

WHAT'S MORE . . .

La bohème is Puccini's most loveable opera—the music is gorgeous, there are no villains, and the characters are easy to like and relate to. But Ruggiero Leoncavallo, composer of *Pagliacci*, did not love Puccini's *La bohème*, and he had a very good reason . . . One afternoon in March of 1893, the two composers, who were friendly acquaintances and fans of each other's work, met in a café. Puccini mentioned that he was at work on "Bohème"; Leoncavallo furiously announced that so was he. The daily papers quickly picked up the story and Puccini was quoted as saying, ultimately, that Leoncavallo could go ahead and write his "Bohème," it wouldn't deter Puccini from writing his own. The outcome is well-known: Leoncavallo's, which appeared a year after Puccini's, has rarely been more than a curiosity, while for millions of opera lovers, Puccini's <u>is</u> *La bohème*.

WHAT TO LISTEN FOR

Act I: Rodolfo's and Mimi's rhapsodic arias of introduction, "Che gelida manina" and "Mi chiamano Mimi." Act II: Musetta's flirtatious "waltz song." Act III: Mimi's touching farewell, "Addio senza rancor."

MODEST MUSSORGSKY

Boris Godunov

Prologue and Four Acts:
First Performance—
St. Petersburg
(Maryinsky) 1874
Libretto by the composer, after
Pushkin's play of the same name
and Karamazin's *History of the
Russian State*

WHERE AND WHEN
Russia and Poland,
1598-1605

WHO'S WHO
**Boris
Godunov,**
Tsar of Russia
(bass)
Grigory, the Pretender Dimitri
(tenor)
Pimen, an old Monk (bass)
Prince Shuisky (tenor)
Marina Mnishek, Polish princess (soprano)
Varlaam, a renegade monk (bass)

WHAT IT'S ABOUT
This is a chronicle of the rise and fall of one Russian
tsar. The way he rose to power—by murdering the infant
tsarevich—haunts him throughout his reign and becomes a
chief contributor to his fall.

WHAT'S HAPPENING
Prologue: Following the murder of the infant Dimitri, the
confused populace urges Boris to take the Imperial throne.
By Act I, Boris has been in power five years, and times have
been hard; even though he has been a diligent ruler, he is
blamed for all problems. Meanwhile, at a monastery, the

novice Grigory learns from Pimen that the murdered tsarevich would now be his same age. Inspired by this, Grigory escapes from the monastery and, in Act II, his role as Pretender has been established. Prince Shuisky tells Boris about the Pretender and then adds to Boris's emotional instability by describing the mystical aura that had surrounded the murdered tsarevich. Could he be, after all, alive? Act III: Princess Marina seeks power for Poland and aims to win the heart of the Pretender. She succeeds and, in Act IV, the opposing forces draw closer to the throne. Boris, now haunted by the evils of his past, passes his rule to his son and then dies—begging for God's forgiveness.

WHAT'S MORE . . .
The machinations of Mussorgsky's Boris make for a wonderful opera plot, but how much of the intrigue is true? Here is some history surrounding the period covered in the opera . . . After Ivan the Terrible's death, Fyodor, his son by his first wife (he had seven), became Tsar. Fyodor was somewhat weak, and his wife's brother, Boris Godunov, soon became the power behind the throne. Ivan's last wife had been sent away with their young son to a monastery, and in 1591, he died; the "official investigation" claimed he accidentally stabbed himself in the throat during an epileptic seizure. But there were others who believed that Boris had him murdered, and still others who felt that the boy escaped the murder attempt. This last theory came to fruition when, in 1603, after Boris had been in power for five years, a pretender to the throne emerged and made his claim in Poland. Boris died suddenly and mysteriously soon after, and his son was named Tsar. This is where the opera ends—but in real life, the son was murdered, and the Pretender ruled as Tsar. However, he, too, was murdered, and Prince Shuisky became Tsar! And it still isn't known whether or not Boris killed the true heir.

WHAT TO LISTEN FOR
Prologue: Boris's Coronation Scene. Act I: Varlaam's song. Act II: Boris's monologue, duet with Shuisky; Clock Scene. Act III: Marina's aria; Marina-Pretender duet. Act IV: Council Hall in the Kremlin—Pimen's monologue and Boris's death scene.

GEORGES BIZET

Carmen

Four Acts, First Performance—Paris
(Opéra Comique), 1875
Libretto by H. Melihac and L. Halévy

WHERE AND WHEN
Seville, Spain, about 1820

WHO'S WHO
Carmen, a gypsy (soprano or mezzo-soprano)
Micaela, a peasant girl (soprano)
Don José, a soldier (tenor)
Escamillo, a toreador (bass)

WHAT IT'S ABOUT
Don José, a young soldier on duty in Seville, has no reason
not to believe he will return to his village, his devoted mother,
and his intended bride Micaela. But he meets the beautiful and
restless Carmen, she tosses him a blood-red flower, and all
innocence disappears in a cloud of gypsy smoke.

WHAT'S HAPPENING
Carmen first appears from a crowd of cigarette factory girls,
besotting every soldier she passes. All except for Don José,
and his very indifference spurs her on to cast her spell. When
she becomes his prisoner following a factory brawl, he allows
her to escape and goes to prison himself. In Act II, while waiting for Don José's release, Carmen flirts with the toreador
Escamillo. She rejects him—but only for the moment. When
Don José appears, she leads him into more military trouble,
and hides him in the mountains with a smugglers' band. At
their camp, in Act III, Don José faces two unexpected visitors:
Escamillo, who declares himself to be Carmen's new lover,
and Micaela, who has come to take him to his dying mother.
The final act brings Don José back to Seville to confront
Carmen. But she now belongs to Escamillo and turns her back
on José's desperate pleas. He pulls a knife. A slave to passion
and revenge, his release can come only with her death.

WHAT'S MORE . . .

When *Carmen* first appeared a century and a quarter ago, it sent shock waves through decent society everywhere. Women were seen fighting and smoking, and the heroine was, quite simply, the most brazen and unrepentently sexual creature to appear on the opera stage until that point. Don José was turned into a criminal and driven to murder by a slut. Well, times have changed. Carmen can be seen as a totally liberated, self-sufficient woman: "Libre elle est née, et libre elle mourra!" she sings in describing herself ("She was born free and will die free"), and she subscribes to no accepted social norms. And José? Obviously a sexually repressed lunatic who had never been out of the clutches of his mother and virginal girlfriend; a man filled with angers and frustrations just waiting to explode. *Plus ça change . . .*

WHAT TO LISTEN FOR

Act I: Carmen's Habanera ("L'amour est un oiseau rebelle");
Act II: Escamillo's "Toreador Song," Don José's "Flower Song" ("La fleur que tu m'avais jeté"); Act III: Micaela's aria; Act IV: Final duet.

PIETRO MASCAGNI

Cavalleria rusticana
(Rustic Chivalry)

One Act: First performance—Rome
(Teatro Costanzi), 1890
Libretto by B. Targioni-Tazzetti and G. Menasci

WHERE AND WHEN
A village in Sicily, late 19th century

WHO'S WHO
Turiddu, a young soldier (tenor)
Santuzza, a village girl (soprano)
Alfio, a village carter (baritone)
Lola, Alfio's wife (mezzo-soprano)
Mamma Lucia, Turiddu's mother (contralto)

WHAT IT'S ABOUT
It is Eastertime in a rustic village, but the passions that erupt
are far from holy. When Turiddu returns from war to find his
beloved Lola now wed to another man, nothing can make him
give her up—neither her married state nor his own involve-
ment with Santuzza, who is pregnant with his child.

WHAT'S HAPPENING
Turiddu serenades Lola outside her own house before dawn.
A bit later, Alfio, unaware of their tryst, looks for Turiddu
elsewhere. Santuzza covers for Turiddu and warns Mamma
Lucia to do the same. After the townspeople have gone to
church, Santuzza begs Turiddu to be kind and return to her,
but he casts her aside. Thus spurned, she tells Alfio about his
wife's betrayal. She instantly regrets her indiscretion, knowing
that a duel will necessarily follow. Alfio and Turiddu fight,
and the ending shadows the beginning, with Santuzza and
Mamma Lucia joined in their concern for Turiddu. But this
time, he is beyond their aid. As the women embrace, a voice
calls out to announce his death.

Most people consider *Cavalleria rusticana*, with its ruthless realism, the epitome of brutality on the opera stage. Consider its
story: a woman scorned gains revenge by seeing to it that her
ex-lover will pay for having an affair with the wife of a local
bully. As the opera draws to a close, Turiddu sings a farewell
to his mother and then goes offstage, where he is killed by
Alfio, out of view. But it could have been worse, considering
what happens at the end of the story upon which the opera is
based: Alfio challenges Turiddu to a duel, and then he throws
dust in his face, momentarily blinding him. While blinded,
Alfio stabs Turiddu in the throat and stomach, and he laughs
at Turiddu's mother, who will now have no son to help her.
The blood burbles out of Turiddu's throat so violently that
he "could not even gasp." Now, *that*'s strong stuff!

WHAT TO LISTEN FOR
Turiddu's serenade: "O Lola"; Easter prayer and Chorus
"Inneggiamo"; Santuzza's aria "Voi lo sapete"; Santuzza-
Turiddu duet "Tu qui Santuzza?"; Turiddu's farewell
"Mamma, quel vino e generoso."

GIOACHINO ROSSINI

La Cenerentola

(Cinderella)

Two Acts: First Performance—Rome
(Teatro Valle), 1817
Libretto by Jacopo Ferretti

WHERE AND WHEN
Salerno, fairy tale time

WHO'S WHO
Cinderella (mezzo-soprano)
Prince Ramiro (tenor)
Don Magnifico, her stepfather (bass)
Dandini, the Prince's valet (baritone)
Alidoro, Prince Ramiro's tutor (bass)

WHAT IT'S ABOUT
The classic story is recognizable—but only just, since almost
everybody is in disguise. Other dissimilarities: there are no
fairies or vehicular pumpkins, no glass slippers, no stepmother

(it's a step*father* who reigns supremely mean). What we do still have are the egalitarian prince, the dreadful stepsisters, and a Cinderella who keeps on turning that other cheek.

WHAT'S HAPPENING

In Act I, Alidoro pays a visit to the seedy castle of Don Magnifico. Since he's disguised as a beggar, the Don's frou-frou daughters, Clorinda and Tisbe, do not receive him. The shabby-but-sweet Cinderella does. Alidoro recommends the girl to his charge, and Prince Ramiro, disguised as Dandini, is charmed. Alidoro returns to outfit Cinderella for Ramiro's ball. Cinderella appears at the palace, masked, dazzling in the finery provided by Alidoro. In Act II, Ramiro, still in disguise, overhears her declare her love for his servant; overjoyed, he asks for her hand. Instead she gives him one of the two bracelets she is wearing and tells him to repeat his offer in the light of day. By that time, Cinderella is back in her rags, and Ramiro, now dressed as himself, shelters from a storm at Don Magnifico's. Ramiro and Cinderella recognize each other, and the matching bracelets seal their love. Back at the palace, she forgives her family and expresses her joy.

WHAT'S MORE . . .

La Cenerentola's opening night was a failure. There was a brutal storm, a baritone who "had the system, when singing, of shouting like a man possessed," and a tenor "whose voice . . . often seemed like a shopful of wrong notes." Even the novelist Stendhal, Rossini's great admirer and first biographer, wrote (when he heard the opera in Paris) that most of the music was contaminated by "the odor of money-grubbing, gutter-minded business-men." Rossini was undaunted. "Fools!" he said to a friend, "It will be fought over by impresarios and even more by *prime donne*." Of course, he was right: By year's end it was staged in seven other Italian cities, and before Rossini died, it saw productions in English, French, Russian, Polish, Czech, and German, in addition to dozens more in Italian. It was the first opera ever staged in Australia. And its abused, loving, forgiving heroine has taken a permanent place in our hearts.

TO LISTEN FOR

Act I: Dandini's aria "Come un ape"; Quintet "Signor, una parola." Act II: Sextet "Questo è un nodo avviluppato"; Cenerentola's Rondo finale "Nacqui all'affanno."

WOLFGANG AMADEUS MOZART

Così fan tutte
(Women Are Like That)

Two Acts: First performance—Vienna
(Burgtheater, 1790)
Libretto by Lorenzo da Ponte

WHERE AND WHEN
Naples, 18th century

WHO'S WHO
Fiordiligi (soprano)
Dorabella, her sister (soprano)
Despina, their maid (soprano)
Ferrando, Dorabella's fiancé (tenor)
Guglielmo, Fiordiligi's fiancé (baritone)
Don Alfonso, elderly philosopher (bass)

WHAT IT'S ABOUT
The two engaged men are complacent about the faithfulness
of their fiancées; the cynical Don Alfonso feels the need to set
them straight. The Don's theory is that all women have a
common problem: they cannot be trusted and, therefore, they
must be tested. Herein lies the story—and the theme of
entangled loyalty and love.

WHAT'S HAPPENING
In Act I, Don Alfonso's plan goes into action: Ferrando and
Guglielmo will pretend to leave for war; in fact, they will reap-
pear in disguise as two Albanians. Don Alfonso recommends
the young men to the ladies, and he is aided by the maid
Despina, who thinks her mistresses should look for amuse-
ment while their lovers are away. The fiancées successfully
fend off the Albanians' attentions until, in Act II, they finally
weaken, with Dorabella falling first, followed with far more
reluctance by Fiordiligi. Just as a double wedding is in the off-
ing, the bridegrooms enter. They are now Ferrando and
Guglielmo, carrying their Albanian disguises. The women
plead for mercy, and the men grant it, with everyone praising
tolerance and agreeing that reason must rule.

WHAT'S MORE . . .

The Emperor himself
had suggested the subject
matter of *Cosi*, which was said
to be based on an incident that
had occurred in Vienna a few months
before. Mozart found da Ponte's libretto
"frivolous and degrading." In August of 1879, while Mozart
was hard at work on *Cosi fan tutte*, he wrote to his wife,
Constanze, who was in Baden, taking the waters, and apparently a bit more: "I do wish that you would sometimes not
make yourself so cheap . . . ," he wrote, "remember that you
yourself once admitted to me that you were inclined to comply too easily." Could he have been taking the situation in
Cosi personally? Whatever the case, the music and understanding transcend any personal dissatisfactions. As always, Mozart
saw all sides of a story, and created music that is at once satiri-
cal and loving, bitter and forgiving. But a question remains: do
the couples return to their original fiancés, or do they stay
together as they have found themselves in the opera?

WHAT TO LISTEN FOR

Act I: Quintet "Sento oh Dio"; Trio "Soave sia il vento";
Fiordiligi's aria "Come scoglio"; Ferrando's aria "Un aura
amorosa." Act II: Ferrando-Guglielmo duet with chorus
"Secondate, aurette amiche"; Guglielmo-Dorabella duet "Il
cor vo dono"; Ferrando-Fiordiligi duet "Fra gli amplessi."

GIUSEPPE VERDI

Don Carlo

Five (Later Four) Acts:
First Five-Act perfor-
mance—Paris (Opéra),
1867; First Four-Act
Performance—Milan
(La Scala), 1884
Libretto by J. Méry
and C. du Locle

WHERE AND WHEN
France and Spain, 1650

WHO'S WHO
Elisabetta de Valois, later to be Queen of Spain (soprano)
Princess Eboli, her lady-in-waiting (mezzo-soprano)
Philip II, King of Spain (bass)
The Infante Don Carlo, his son and heir to the Spanish
throne (tenor)
Rodrigo, his friend (baritone)
The Grand Inquisitor (bass)

WHAT IT'S ABOUT
Don Carlo and the French noblewoman Elisabetta fall in love,
only to learn that she must become the bride of his father.
Personal jealousies and political intrigue thrust Carlo into
conflict with his father and the Church, distancing him ever
further from the woman he loves.

WHAT'S HAPPENING
In Act I, Don Carlo goes to France to claim Elisabetta,
promised to him as part of a peace treaty. They are delighted
to discover that this arranged marriage will also be a union of
love; however, their ecstasy is short-lived: King Philip declares
that he will take his son's place at the altar. Back in Spain in
Act II, Rodrigo tries to help Don Carlo with both his political and romantic endeavors. He bungles a message and mis-
leads Princess Eboli into thinking it is she Carlo loves.
Rodrigo also confers with the King, believing he can influence

his thinking and further Don Carlo's causes. Act III brings a secret meeting between Carlo and the woman he thinks is Elisabetta. It is in fact Eboli, who realizes that Carlo loves his stepmother and threatens to betray them to the King. In the meantime, Flemish Protestants are about to be burned at the stake. When Carlo sides with them, the King declares this to be treason. Rodrigo, to all appearances a turncoat, disarms Carlo and wins Philip's favor. During Act IV, the lonely King Philip uncovers the love affair between his wife and his imprisoned son. Then the scene changes to Carlo's dungeon, where Rodrigo shows up, prepared to take the blame for the Flemish fiasco so that Carlo can be released and pardoned. Before this can happen, Rodrigo is shot, and the King arrives to offer his son freedom on royal terms. Carlo refuses and, in Act V, escapes to the monastery where his grandfather, Emperor Charles V, is entombed. Elisabetta is there as well, and she and Carlo share what they think is a last embrace. However, when the King and The Inquisitor arrive to make their arrest, Charles V (or a monk in disguise) materializes and leads Carlo into the cloister's safe haven.

WHAT'S MORE . . .

So much has been written about the various versions of *Don Carlo* (French [*Don Carlos*], Italian, five act, four act), that we need not go over it again here. Rather, take note of the character of Don Carlo himself, Verdi's strangest hero. Verdi gives him only one brief solo—we get to know him through his duet with Rodrigo, his three with Elisabetta, one with Eboli, and so forth. We like him, and we feel his plight: he wants to love Elisabetta but he isn't permitted, he wants to be a political hero but he hasn't the strength or wherewithal. The historic Don Carlo was a slightly deformed, slightly retarded misfit. Verdi and his librettists have turned him into a hero, although he remains an unfulfilled hero to the end.

WHAT TO LISTEN FOR

Act I: Carlo-Elisabetta duet "Di qual amor." Act II: Carlo-Rodrigo duet "Dio, nell'alma infondere"; Eboli's "Veil Song"; Carlo-Elisabetta duet "Io vengo a domandar." Act III: 1st scene duet/trio - Carlo, Eboli/Rodrigo; Auto-da-fé scene. Act IV: Philip's aria "Ella giammai m'amo"; Philip-Grand Inquisitor duet; Eboli's aria "O don fatale"; Rodrigo's death scene . . . Act V: Elisabetta's aria "Tu che le vanità."

JACQUES OFFENBACH

Les Contes d'Hoffmann

(The Tales of Hoffmann)

Prologue, Three Acts and Epilogue: First Performance,
Paris, 1881
Libretto by J. Barbier and M. Carré, based on stories by
the poet E.T.A. Hoffmann

WHERE AND WHEN
Nuremberg, 19th century

WHO'S WHO
Hoffmann, a poet (tenor)
Nicklausse, his companion (mezzo-soprano)
Stella, a prima donna; **Olympia,** a doll; **Giulietta,** a courtesan;
Antonia, a young woman (all sopranos)
Lindorf, Coppelius, Miracle, Dapertutto—Hoffmann's
nemeses (bass/baritone)

WHAT IT'S ABOUT
The poet Hoffmann tells three stories to his friends. Each is
about a former love, and is a poetic metaphor for a stage in
Hoffmann's search for Art.

WHAT'S HAPPENING
Prologue: Hoffmann enters a tavern to wait for Stella, his cur-
rent amour. The entrance of Lindorf, who also loves Stella,
reminds Hoffmann of old loves and old rivals. His stories
begin. Act I: Hoffmann is fooled into believing that Olympia,
a doll, is real, until she is destroyed by Coppelius, leaving
Hoffmann heartbroken and ridiculed. Act II has either of two
endings following Giulietta's "theft" (engineered by the sinis-
ter Dapertutto) of Hoffmann's reflection: in one, she drinks
poison intended for Hoffmann and dies; in the other, she is
carried off in a gondola by an admirer. Act III: Antonia, the
young recluse, must never sing, lest she follow in the footsteps
of her mother, a mezzo who sang herself to death. Hoffmann
can't keep her from her fate—at the hands of Dr. Miracle—
and he loses his third love. Epilogue: Back at the tavern,

Hoffmann is both downhearted and drunk. Stella arrives, finds him incoherent and exits with Lindorf. Hoffmann forswears women in favor of his Muse.

WHAT'S MORE . . .

Because Offenbach died before completing "Hoffmann," and since new, previously unseen manuscript pages have been turning up recently in abundance (over 1600 of them in the 1970s, an additional 350 in 1984), much is made of which edition is the "correct" one and would best show us the composer's intentions. There are recordings available of at least four versions; the opera keeps changing as pieces are added and subtracted. As early as 1904, "helpers" were adding music from other Offenbach works as well: Dapertutto's aria, "Scintille, diamant" is from the composer's *Le voyage dans la lune*, and the famous septet, "Hélas, mon coeur," was composed by a stranger— André Bloch—based on themes from the famous barcarolle that opens the Venice act. And the barcarolle itself? Borrowed by Offenbach from his own earlier opera, *Les fées du Rhin*!

WHAT TO LISTEN FOR

Prologue: Hoffmann's song "Il était une fois à la cour d'Eisenach." Act I: Doll Song (Olympia) "Les oiseaux dans la charmille." Act II: Barcarolle; Dapertutto's aria "Scintille, diamant"; Hoffmann's aria "O Dieu, de quelle ivresse." Act III: Antonia's aria "Elle a fui . . ."; Hoffmann-Antonia duet "C'est une chanson d'amour"; trio - Dr Miracle, Antonia, voice of Antonia's mother "Ta mère? Oses-tu l'invoquer?"

WOLFGANG AMADEUS MOZART

Don Giovanni

Two Acts, First Performance—Prague (National),
1787   Libretto by Lorenzo da Ponte

WHERE AND WHEN
Seville, Spain, 17th century

WHO'S WHO
Don Giovanni, a young nobleman (baritone)
Leporello, his servant (bass or baritone)
The Commendatore (bass)
Donna Anna, his daughter (soprano)
Don Ottavio, betrothed to Donna Anna (tenor)
Donna Elvira, a lady of Burgos (soprano)
Zerlina, a country maiden (soprano or mezzo-soprano)
Masetto, her betrothed (baritone)

WHAT IT'S ABOUT
Don Giovanni is the portrait of a man you love to hate. Based
on the legendary character of Don Juan Tenorio, this
Giovanni is sometimes scandalous, sometimes endearing,
always maddening. He leaves a trail of heartbroken women
and angry threats from their men, but he laughs everything off
and strikes again. Refusing to reform or repent, Giovanni dies
to uphold his motto: *long live women, long live wine, the strength and
glory of mankind.*

WHAT'S HAPPENING
We first encounter Don Giovanni making a hurried exit from
the house of Donna Anna, his most recent amorous target,
assisted by his servant, Leporello. After the Don wins a fatal
duel (with Anna's father the Commentadore), insults a former
amoureuse (Donna Elvira), and schemes to seduce a young
peasant bride-to-be (Zerlina), the injured parties rally themselves to bring the scoundrel down. However, in Act II, Don
Giovanni unintentionally beats them to it. He flippantly issues
a dinner invitation to the memorial statue of the dead
Commentadore. When the statue arrives for the banquet, he
challenges his host to "think upon your sins and repent." The

Don answers with an emphatic "No," even as he is dragged into the flames of hell.

WHAT'S MORE . . .

Is *Don Giovanni* a "dramma giocoso" (playful drama) as it is designated in both score and libretto, or "opera buffa" (comic opera) as Mozart referred to it in his own catalog? It is designed to be both. The overture, for example, begins in a dark, minor mode and proceeds into lighthearted, witty merriment. At the opera's end, the double finale provides further proof. The first part shows the corrupt, immoral Don dragged to hell for refusing to repent; its second part consists of an upbeat sextet in which the other characters decide what they will do with the rest of their lives. In the 19th century, moralistic audiences preferred that the second part of the finale be omitted, making the opera far more "dramma" than "giocoso" or "buffa" and thereby doing Mozart a disservice. He wanted a fusion of tragic and comic, darkness and light, and he achieved it from beginning to end, as no other composer could. The result is what is often considered to be the greatest opera ever written.

TO LISTEN FOR

Act I: Leporello's Catalog aria, in which he describes all of the Don's conquests; the seductive duet "La ci darem la mano" between Don Giovanni and Zerlina; Donna Anna's "Or sai chi l'onore," where she demands revenge against the Don.
Act II: The Don's serenade, "Deh, vieni;" the sextet "Solo, solo in buio loco;" Don Ottavio's "Il mio tesoro," in which he promises to avenge Donna Anna; double finale.

GAETANO DONIZETTI

L'Elisir d'amore

(The Elixir of Love)

Two Acts: First Performance, Milan (Teatro della Canobbiana), 1832
Libretto by Felice Romani

WHERE AND WHEN
An Italian village, early 19th century

WHO'S WHO
Adina, richest girl in the village (soprano)
Nemorino, her poor admirer (tenor)
Dulcamara, a quack doctor (bass)
Belcore, a swaggering soldier (baritone)

WHAT IT'S ABOUT
A sleepy village wakes up when a medicine man sets up shop.
He promises a magic cure for unrequited love, and sure
enough, the right boy does get the girl. Was the magic nothing more than false courage? This ending is so happy that no
one really cares.

WHAT'S HAPPENING
In Act I, Nemorino, mooning over Adina as usual, droops in
defeat when the dashing Belcore appears. He rushes to the
quack Dulcamara and spends all his money on an elixir that
guarantees love. It's really only wine. Nemorino gulps it down,
and his drunken antics drive Adina into a hasty acceptance of
Belcore's proposal. Act II, and it's almost wedding time.
Nemorino needs more elixir, so he signs up for the army to
get quick cash. In the meantime, his rich uncle has died, leaving our hero a rich man. The village girls swoon, and
Nemorino, thinking it's the potion, courts Adina with new-
found charm. She spurns Belcore, gets Nemorino out of the
army, and gives her heart to the right man at last.

WHAT'S MORE . . .
Conditions of opera composition—and performance— were
very different in the opera-rich Italy of the 19th century.
When Donizetti accepted the difficult challenge of compos-

ing an opera in less than a month for the Cannobiana Theatre
in Milan (the management had been suddenly let down by
another composer), he immediately turned to the fine librett-
tist, Felice Romani, for help. He wrote "I give you a week . . .
Bear in mind we have a German prima donna, a tenor who
stammers, a buffo with a voice like a goat and a French bass
who isn't worth much . . . " And when the composer Berlioz
attended a performance of the opera in the third week of its
run, he recorded the following in his "Memoirs": "I found the
theatre full of people talking in normal voices, their backs to
the stage. The singers, undeterred, gesticulated and yelled their
lungs out . . . People were gambling, eating supper in their
boxes, etc." Times have changed!

WHAT TO LISTEN FOR

Act I: Nemorino-Adina duet "Chiedi all'aura"; Dulcamara's
aria "Udite, udite o rustii."
Act II: Nemorino's aria "Una furtiva lagrima."

PETER ILYICH TCHAIKOVSKY

Eugene Onegin

Three Acts: First professional performance—Moscow (Bolshoi), 1881
Libretto by composer and K. Shilovsky, after Pushkin's poem of same name

WHERE AND WHEN
The Russian countryside and St. Petersburg, late 18th century

WHO'S WHO
Tatiana (soprano)
Olga, her sister (mezzo-soprano)
Lenski, Olga's suitor (tenor)
Eugene Onegin, his friend (baritone)
Prince Gremin (bass)

WHAT IT'S ABOUT
The disdainful and vain Onegin spurns the love offered by the young and dreamy Tatiana. Much later, when she has blossomed into a beautiful woman, he changes his mind and pur-

sues her. However, his brashness has caused too much tragedy in the intervening years. He is doomed to live with his past mistakes.

WHAT'S HAPPENING

In Act I, left in the background by her sister's engagement to Lenski, Tatiana declares her love for Onegin in a flowery letter. At their next meeting, he chides her for her impetuous behavior. Act II brings a gala ball given by the sisters' mother. Onegin shows up, in bad temper, and spends his time flirting with Olga. Lenski objects, and the two friends duel. After the pistols have been fired, Lenski is dead. Act III. Years later, in St. Petersburg, Onegin attends another ball, but without gaiety: his guilty conscience has dogged his days. Then Prince Gremin introduces his lovely wife, and she is Tatiana. Onegin feels a sudden rush of passion for her, as well as hope for a new and better life. His hopes soar when she admits she still loves him; however, she now has the very control over her emotions he once admonished her for lacking. She will never give in.

WHAT'S MORE . . .

While Tchaikovsky was at work on *Eugene Onegin*, a young student named Antonina was courting him; indeed, she was begging him to marry her. He certainly didn't want to behave like the too-worldly, cold, eventually rueful Onegin, and ashamed of and perplexed by his homosexuality, he finally gave in. The marriage was a catastrophe, and he fled at once, following up with a nervous breakdown and a suicide attempt. (If the truth be known, Tchaikovsky was never stable: early in his career, while conducting, he got the impression that his head was about to fall off and he led the rest of the performance with one hand supporting it.) The opera, as we know, ends with Tatiana rejecting Onegin; real life was somewhat different. Antonina pleaded and threatened blackmail for years; she was finally committed to an insane asylum where she spent the rest of her life.

WHAT TO LISTEN FOR

Act I: Tatiana's letter scene "Puskai pogibnu ya . . . ";
Onegin-Tatiana duet "Zdyes on, Zdyes on, Yevgeni!"
Act II: Lenski's aria "Kuda, kuda, kuda vi udalilis."
Act III: Gremin's aria "Lyubvi vsye vozrasti pokorni";
final duet - Onegin-Tatiana "O! Kak mnye tyazhelo."

GIACOMO PUCCINI

La fanciulla del west

(*The Girl of the Golden West*)

Three Acts: First Performance, New York
(Metropolitan), 1910
Libretto by C. Zangarini and G. Civinini

WHERE AND WHEN

California mining camp during the Gold Rush: 1849-1850

WHO'S WHO

Minnie, saloon-keeper, Bible teacher (soprano)
Dick Johnson, a.k.a. the bandit Ramerrez (tenor)
Jack Rance, sheriff (baritone)

WHAT IT'S ABOUT

Puccini takes us to the Cloudy Mountains of California, for
this Italian salute to the American West. In doing so, he also
gives us the memorable Minnie, a heroine who brings out the
best in a bunch of rowdy men.

WHAT'S HAPPENING

Act I: Dick Johnson, a newcomer, swings his way into the
Polka Saloon. Minnie, who has met him briefly before, falls
for him on the spot. Rance, who wants Minnie for his own,
suspects that Dick is really Ramerrez, a bandit on the lam. In
Act II, Dick Johnson/Ramerrez visits Minnie in her cabin,
and she discovers his real identity. She tells him to leave, and
when he does and gets wounded by the sheriff's posse, the
lovestruck Minnie hides him in her loft. Meanwhile, she challenges Rance to a poker game with Johnson as the prize. She
cheats and wins; Rance retreats. However, in Act III, Johnson
has been captured anyway. He is about to be hanged when
Minnie gallops up, makes the miners realize all she has done
for them, and saves Johnson—this time, for good.

WHAT'S MORE . . .

La fanciulla del west is Puccini's least Puccini-like opera, that is, it relies less on set pieces and catchy melodies than it does on inventive touches. The first act offers Debussy-like, impressionistic orchestration; the second-act poker scene finds the soprano and baritone barely singing (so stifling is the tension) against a background of pizzicato double-basses; and the third act goes out with a whisper, both vocally and orchestrally. Despite these oddities—or perhaps because of them— Maurice Ravel found the score extraordinary and instructed his pupils to study it, and Richard Strauss said he would like to have composed the second act. And the audience at the world premiere in New York loved it too: Puccini was present, Caruso and Emmy Destinn sang, Toscanini conducted, and there were more than 50 curtain calls at the end.

WHAT TO LISTEN FOR

Act I: Rance-Minnie scene—"Minnie, dalla mia casa . . . "
Act II: Johnson's aria "Una parola sola!"; Poker Scene finale.
Act III: Johnson's aria "Ch'ella mi creda."

CHARLES GOUNOD

Faust

Five Acts: First performance—Paris
(Théâtre Lyrique), 1859
Libretto by Jules Barbier

WHERE AND WHEN
Germany, 16th century

WHO'S WHO
Faust, an aged philosopher (tenor)
Méphistophélès (bass)
Marguerite (soprano)
Valentin, her brother (baritone)

WHAT IT'S ABOUT
Faust sells his soul to the devil for a two-pronged payoff: a
return to youth and the love of innocent Marguerite. No good
can come from this evil plan, but there is at least some heaven-
ly intervention at the very end.

WHAT'S HAPPENING
In Act I, the aging Faust is ripe for Méphistophélès, who
offers his tempting contract. As soon as Faust signs it, he is
young again, and he leaves with the devil to snare Marguerite.
In Acts II and III, unable to resist either the jewels or the spell
Méphistophélès produces, she falls into the arms of Faust. By
Act IV, Faust has deserted her, even though she is carrying his
child. Overcome with shame, she enters a church to repent.
Now after *her* soul as well, Méphistophélès sends a chorus of
demons to vie with the choir. Faust duels with Marguerite's
outraged brother, Valentin, who dies by Faust's fiendishly-
guided sword. In Act V, in the midst of bacchanalean revels,
Faust sees a vision of Marguerite, imprisoned for the murder
of her child. He goes to her, accompanied, as ever, by
Méphistophélès. Seeing them together, she realizes the evil
complicity and calls on angels to save her. They bear her
toward heaven as she dies.

WHAT'S MORE . . .

The Faust legend fascinates people, and has for centuries. There *was* a Dr. Faust living in Knittingen from 1480 to 1540, and he was known as a magician of sorts, a sorcerer. He was mentioned in sermons by German Protestant reformers in 1550 and after, and late in the century, Christopher Marlowe wrote the *Tragical History of Doctor Faustus*. After Marlowe there were occasional mentions, but Goethe put the old Doctor on the map for good, beginning in 1808. Valéry and Thomas Mann soon followed, and, in art, Rembrandt and Delacroix took up the legend. In music there have been Schubert, Berlioz, Liszt, Boito, Spohr, Wagner, Mahler, Busoni and others—but Gounod's opera is the most popular incarnation. The story remains riveting because of the character of Doctor Faust himself: In the Reformation days of hellfire and brimstone, this man was willing to risk it all—and that makes him both alluring and appalling.

WHAT TO LISTEN FOR

Act I: Faust-Méphistophélès duet "A moi les plaisirs!" Act II: Valentin's aria "Avant de quitter ces lieux"; Méphistophélès' aria "Le veau d'or." Act III: Faust's aria "Salut demeure"; Marguerite's aria "Il était un Roi de Thulé . . . O Dieu que de bijoux!"; Marguerite-Faust duet "Il se fait tard!" Act IV: Church scene—Marguerite, chorus, Méphistophélès—"Seigneur, daignez permettre"; Soldier's Chorus "Gloire immortelle." Act V: Prison scene duet— Marguerite-Faust—and final trio "Oui, c'est moi, je t'aime! . . . Alerte! Alerte! Anges purs!"

LUDWIG VAN BEETHOVEN

Fidelio

Two Acts: (For performance facts, see "What's More" on opposite page.)
Libretto by Joseph von Sonnleithner

WHERE AND WHEN
Seville, 18th century

WHO'S WHO
Leonora, in disguise as Fidelio (soprano)
Florestan, her husband, a Spanish nobleman (tenor)
Pizarro, prison governor (baritone)
Rocco, jailer (bass)
Marcellina, his daughter (soprano)

WHAT IT'S ABOUT
Florestan is supposed to be dead, but he is actually a political prisoner, held secretly by Pizarro in his fortress jail. Leonora alone suspects the truth and, eventually, sets her husband free. Her determination, faithfulness, and willingness to face any danger tell the story of married love triumphant over all.

WHAT'S HAPPENING
In Act I, Leonora, in disguise as the young man Fidelio, has taken a job as helper to Rocco. She easily wins favor with him; unfortunately, her appeal spreads to Marcellina as well. An unfortunate situation, but Leonora perseveres, having learned that Florestan is confined in the deepest dungeon cell. Her mission becomes even more urgent when Pizarro, nervous at the pending arrival of the Minister of State, announces he will kill Florestan and bury him to destroy the evidence. Act II opens upon Florestan, chained in his cell. Nearby are Rocco and Fidelio, digging the grave. Pizarro enters and draws his dagger, but Fidelio pulls out a stolen pistol and steps between the two men. She cries, to everyone's surprise, "First kill his wife!" The Minister arrives on the scene, recognizes his old friend Florestan, and gives Fidelio/Leonora the honor of freeing her husband from his bonds.

WHAT'S MORE . . .

Fidelio, Beethoven's only opera, had a very long, difficult birth—rather, series of births. Its first version premiered in 1805 but was unsatisfactory; it was quickly withdrawn and revised. In 1806 a second version appeared, with two, rather than three acts, and in 1814, the version we know today was presented. The first two versions, rarely performed, are customarily referred to as *Leonore*. To add to the confusion, there are four overtures: *Leonore No. 2*, which was composed first and performed at the premiere; *Leonore No. 3*, which is occasionally inserted before the opera's final scene (and opened the opera at its 1806 revision); *Fidelio*, which was composed for 1814 and now always begins the opera; and *Leonore No. 1*, composed for a planned Prague production but dropped. Each (except for the unperformed #1) bears the stamp of Beethoven's passionate devotion to the concept of freedom; each rings with the urgency of his ninth symphony.

WHAT TO LISTEN FOR

Act I: Leonore's aria "Abscheulicher!"
Act II: Florestan's aria "Gott! Welch Dunkel hier!"; the quartet "Er sterbe!"

JOHANN STRAUSS

Die Fledermaus
(The Bat)

Three Acts: First Performance, Vienna
(an der Wein), 1874
Libretto by C. Haffner and R. Genée

WHERE AND WHEN
Vienna, circa 1850

WHO'S WHO
Rosalinde (soprano)
Adele, her maid (soprano)
Eisenstein, her husband (tenor)
Alfred, her lover (tenor)
Prince Orlofsky (mezzo-soprano)
Dr. Falke (baritone)

WHAT IT'S ABOUT
Dr. Falke sets into motion perhaps the most convoluted and
confounding of all operatic practical jokes. The question is
not *What is it about,* but *Who are these masked people?*

WHAT'S HAPPENING

In Act I, Falke wants to get even for a humiliating joke played on him following a party, wherein he woke up in broad daylight dressed as a bat. He invites the perpetrator, Eisenstein, to a party, and plans some humiliations of his own. Eisenstein tells Rosalinde he's off to serve a pending jail sentence (which he ought to be doing), but he's really heading for the party. That leaves Rosalinde home alone with Alfred, and when the prison governor arrives, he mistakes her lover for her husband and takes him off to jail. Act II, at Prince Orlofsky's party, everyone wears masks and gets befuddled, including the maid Adele and, most of all, Eisenstein, who flirts wildly with a woman he doesn't recognize as his wife. Act III unfolds in and around the jail, where true identities come to light and indiscretions are forgiven, with everything blamed on the revenge of the bat.

WHAT'S MORE . . .

Meilhac and Halévy were the writers who supplied Jacques Offenbach with some of his most memorable texts, and when Johann Strauss came upon what was to turn into *Die Fledermaus* (a French play by the pair called *Le réveillon*), his place in operatic history was assured. *Fledermaus* is a light opera that has always attracted the "heaviest" of singers and conductors; unlike some other operettas, which can be "thrown together" by a sincere semi-professional troupe, real pros are needed to perform it effectively. It was a favorite of conductors Gustav Mahler, Richard Strauss, Bruno Walter and Herbert von Karajan, and some of the singers of the past who have found the music and situations irresistible have been Lotte Lehmann, Maria Jeritza, Ernestine Schumann-Heink, Elisabeth Schumann, Eberhard Wächter, Hilde Güden, Rita Streich and Walter Berry. And as long as there are singers with wit and elegance, the champagne will keep flowing!

WHAT TO LISTEN FOR

Act I: Trio "So muss allein ich bleiben." Act II: Adele's aria "Mein Herr Marquis"; Rosalinde's aria *Csardas* "Klänge der Heimat." Act III: Trio "Ich stehe voll Sagen."

RICHARD WAGNER

Der fliegende Holländer

(The Flying Dutchman)

One Act (occasionally performed in three acts):
First Performance—Dresden, 1843
Libretto by the composer

WHERE AND WHEN
Norway, 18th century

WHO'S WHO
Holländer, the Dutchman (bass-baritone)
Daland, Captain of a Norwegian ship (bass)
Senta, his daughter (soprano)
Erik, Senta's suitor (tenor)

WHAT IT'S ABOUT
The Dutchman was a legend in his own time. Having made a
foolish oath, he has raised the wrath of Satan and is doomed
to sail the seas forever. There is one hope for his salvation: a
woman who will be true to him until death. The curse allows
him to go ashore every seven years in search of such a woman.
Until he meets Senta, his hopes are as black as the ship he
sails.

WHAT'S HAPPENING
In Scene 1, Daland and the Dutchman, both sea captains,
make a deal when they see the mutual advantages of Daland's
marriageable daughter. Scene 2 introduces Senta, who day-
dreams about the mysterious Dutchman and longs to be the
woman who will set him free. Erik warns her of the danger,
but when her father introduces her to the Dutchman, they fall
in love, and she pledges herself to him until death. In Scene 3,
the Dutchman sees Senta with Erik and mistakenly believes
she has gone back on her word. Wishing to save her from a
second curse—that any unfaithful woman who joins him will
be condemned as well—he sets sail alone. She sees his ship
depart and flings herself into the sea. Her faithfulness thus
proclaimed, the ship sinks, and the spirits of Senta and the
Dutchman rise from the waters, heaven-bound.

WHAT'S MORE . . .

The story of the Flying Dutchman— a sailor doomed to sail the seas forever— was immensely popular in Europe in the first part of the 19th century. Wagner had read Heinrich Heine's "Memoirs of Herr von Schnabelewopski" (1834), in chapter seven of which the title character attends a play about the Dutchman. But there is a good chance that Heine himself had seen a play of the same name by Edward Fitzball which was produced in 1826. And Fitzball had probably read an anonymous story on the subject in a magazine in 1821. Then, in 1839, a novel by Captain Marryat appeared called "The Phantom Ship," about a Dutch sea captain . . . etc. At any rate, after Wagner's opera appeared in 1843, with Heine's setting changed from Scotland to Norway and the concept of a woman's sacrifice through death deepened, it ended the rash of doomed-sea-captain tales, and ever since, when we think of such a character, it is invariably in Wagner's incarnation.

WHAT TO LISTEN FOR

Dutchman's entrance scene "Die Frist ist um . . . "; Senta's ballad "Johohohoe! Traft ihr das Schiff . . . "; Chorus of Norwegian and Dutch sailors; Final scene "Verloren! Ach, verloren!"

AMILCARE PONCHIELLI

La Gioconda

(The Joyful Girl)

Four Acts: First Performance—Milan (La Scala), 1876
Libretto by Arrigo Boito (writing as "Tobia Gorrio")

WHERE AND WHEN
Venice, 17th century

WHO'S WHO
La Gioconda, a street singer (soprano)
Enzo Grimaldo, the Genoese nobleman she loves (tenor)
La Cieca, Gioconda's blind mother (contralto)
Alvise Badoero, a leader of the state Inquisition
Laura, his wife, in lover with Enzo (mezzo-soprano)
Barnaba, a spy, admirer of Gioconda (baritone)

WHAT IT'S ABOUT
Gioconda is a busy grand-opera heroine, with actions that
keep both the plot and the other characters trotting along
apace. Although she has some dark moments in her struggle
to wrest Enzo from her rival Laura, love wins out over murder—every time.

WHAT'S HAPPENING
Act I opens on a festive street scene. Barnaba woos Gioconda,
and when she spurns him, he denounces her mother as a
witch. Gioconda pleads with Alvise for mercy, and Laura
(wearing a mask) kindly intercedes. During the excitement,
Gioconda's beloved Enzo appears, in disguise to foil his enemies. He recognizes Laura, his youthful love, who was forced
to marry his arch-enemy Alvise. In Act II, Barnaba has
arranged a shipboard rendezvous between Laura and Enzo,
hoping to get rid of Enzo for good by revealing all to Alvise.
Gioconda learns of the meeting and sneaks aboard prepared to
kill for love. However, when she sees that Laura is the woman
who saved her mother, she helps her rival escape. By Act III,
Alvise has learned of Laura's unfaithfulness and commands
her to take poison. Before she can, Gioconda substitutes a
sleeping draught and, in Act IV, to free the imprisoned Enzo,
she promises herself to Barnaba in exchange. She contem-

plates another attempt to do away with Laura, but changes her mind and arranges safe passage for the lovers. She then kills herself before Barnaba can claim her.

WHAT'S MORE . . .

Opera doesn't get much grander than *La Gioconda*. The first act takes place in the courtyard of the Doge's Palace in Venice; the second act, set at sea, offers a ship in flames; the third act is set in a room and then a ballroom in the *Ca d'oro* (the "house of gold"—one of the most sumptuous 15th century palaces in Venice), and the final act calls for no less than a ruined palace on an island. In addition, six top-notch singers are required—one in each major voice category—and, of course, there's the third-act ballet ("Dance of the Hours," re-animated by Disney in the movie *Fantasia*). The music is tuneful and accessible, the action almost non-stop—what more could anyone want? Well, here's a hint: the great American dramatic soprano Lillian Nordica, after she had sung the title role nearly seventy five times, confessed that she had no idea what the opera was about! The librettist Boito, better known for Verdi's *Otello* and *Falstaff* libretti, used a pen name for *La Gioconda*. A wise career move, perhaps?

WHAT TO LISTEN FOR

Act I: Enzo - Barnaba duet; Barnaba's aria "O monumento!"
Act II: Enzo's aria "Cielo e mar"; Enzo-Laura duet ; Laura-Gioconda duet "E un anatema!" Act III: Alvise-Laura duet ; ensemble "Gia ti veggo, immota e smorta." Act IV: Gioconda's aria - "Suicidio!"

ENGELBERT HUMPERDINCK

Hänsel und Gretel

Three Acts: First Performance, Weimar,
Christmas 1893
Libretto by Adelheid Wette

WHERE AND WHEN
German mountains, legendary time

WHO'S WHO
Hänsel (mezzo-soprano)
Gretel, his sister (soprano)
Witch (mezzo-soprano)
Sandman, Dew Fairy (two sopranos)
Gertrud, their mother (soprano)
Peter, their father, a broommaker (baritone)

WHAT IT'S ABOUT
The story is little changed
from the well-known
Grimm Brothers tale,
with clever children
outwitting the can-
nibalistic witch,
and a house
that's so deli-
cious it may
be the most
memorable
"character"
of all.

WHAT'S HAPPENING

In Act I, Peter returns home to hear that Gertrud has unwittingly sent Hänsel and Gretel into the witch's woods. In Act II, the children realize they are lost, and they are frightened until the Sandman appears with his blessing of sleep. Act III brings the dawn and the Dew Fairy, but soon the children are on their own. They can't resist the gingerbread house that has appeared before their eyes. When they begin to nibble, the witch invites them in and casts her spell. Gretel breaks it by finding the witch's magic wand, and she and Hänsel push the witch into her own oven—just what she was planning to do to them! The oven explodes, the gingerbread fence turns back into children, and the parents arrive in time to share a big witch cake.

WHAT'S MORE . . .

In *Hänsel und Gretel*, Humperdinck blends an uncanny mixture of Wagnerian technique with a type of folksiness and naiveté that make the opera unique. Its genesis might explain the contradictions: the libretto was written by Adelheid Wette, who lived in Cologne with her husband and two daughters. Adelheid's younger brother, Max, built a puppet theatre for the girls and they put on plays, many based on Grimm's fairy tales, with texts by Adelheid. The girls loved to sing, too, so Adelheid asked her older brother to set her lines to music, which he did, occasionally using folk tunes. This older brother had worked as an assistant on the first performance of Wagner's *Parsifal*—and his name was Engelbert Humperdinck. What he turned out, with his nieces' and sister's help, was an opera that was translated into 11 languages within a few years of its premiere: a post-Wagnerian composition with an innocent touch, and an opera for sophisticates and novices alike.

WHAT TO LISTEN FOR

Act I: Duet "Brüderchen, komm, tanz mit mir." Act II: Sandman's song and Hänsel and Gretel's song "Abends will ich schlafen gehn." Act III: Witch's spell "Hokus, pokus, Hexenschuss!"

RICHARD WAGNER

Lohengrin

Three Acts: First Performance, Weimar, 1850
Libretto by the composer

WHERE AND WHEN
Antwerp, 10th century

WHO'S WHO
Lohengrin (tenor)
Elsa, Princess of Brabant (soprano)
Friedrich von Telramund, her uncle and guardian (baritone)
Ortrud, his pagan wife (mezzo-soprano)
Heinrich, King of Germany (bass)

WHAT IT'S ABOUT

The moral: don't ask shining knights too many questions. Elsa learns this too late, and her curiosity—fed by the evil Ortrud—destroys a perfect love.

WHAT'S HAPPENING

In Act I, Elsa is blamed unjustly for the mysterious disappearance of her brother. Her innocence or guilt will be decided by combat, but there is no one to champion her side. Then, in a riverboat drawn by a swan, a knight in silver armor appears, offering to be both her protector and her future husband. She accepts and promises to obey his one command: she must never ask his name or his history. Act II spotlights Ortrud and Friedrich. They have already stolen the dukedom belonging to Elsa's brother and now must rout the popular knight by spreading rumors about his past. Their stories feed Elsa's curiosity, and in Act III, she asks the forbidden questions to her brand new groom. When Friedrich breaks in, Lohengrin kills him and declares that he must go before the King to answer the questions asked by his bride. What Lohengrin reveals is that he is a Knight of the Holy Grail. He then transforms his swan into the human form of Elsa's brother, a victim of Ortrud's spell. All rejoice, but too soon: Lohengrin, exposed, must now vanish, and Elsa dies in her brother's arms.

WHAT'S MORE . . .

In 1845, an overwrought (as usual) Richard Wagner, having just completed his opera *Tannhäuser*, was instructed by his physician to go to Marienbad Spa to take the water cure, and by no means to allow himself to get upset. He brought with him an anonymous epic about Lohengrin, son of the knight Parzival, which he read while communing with nature. As he later reported . . . one day he took the book with him into the medicinal baths, and it was there, in complete relaxation, that he had a vision of how to treat the story operatically. He left the bath immediately and returned to his rooms where he wrote the synopsis of *Lohengrin*—in almost the exact form we know today.

WHAT TO LISTEN FOR

Act I: Elsa's dream "Einsam in truben Tagen."
Act II: Elsa-Ortrud scene "Euch luften . . . "
Act III: Prelude, Bridal Chorus, Lohengrin's narrative "In fernem land."

GAETANO DONIZETTI

Lucia di Lammermoor

Three Acts: First Performance—Naples
(Teatro San Carlo), 1835
Libretto by Salvatore Cammarano
An early Romantic opera, based on Sir Walter Scott's
novel, *The Bride of Lammermoor*

WHERE AND WHEN
Scotland, 1695

WHO'S WHO
Lucia (soprano)
Edgardo, her lover (tenor)
Enrico, Lucia's brother (baritone)
Raimondo, the chaplain (bass)

WHAT IT'S ABOUT
The love of Lucia and Edgardo is doomed from the start.
He is a Ravenswood, and she is an Ashton. Not since the
Capulets and the Montagues have there been two more
warring families, and the cruel scheming of her kin drives
Lucia mad.

WHAT'S HAPPENING
In Act I, Enrico wants to recapture the Ashton family fortune
glory and gain political favor by marrying off Lucia to the
wealthy Arturo. However, unknown to her brother, Lucia has
promised herself to Edgardo. Her secret comes to light in Act
II, when Enrico discovers the letters from her lover and forges
one to convince her that Edgardo is unfaithful. Aghast at this
revelation and urged on by a trusted chaplain, Lucia reluctantly agrees to an unhappy marriage with Arturo. Edgardo
appears just as she is signing the contract and denounces her.
In Act III, Lucia emerges from her wedding chamber raving
and spattered with blood. She has murdered Arturo and is
dying herself. In the final scene, hearing the bell toll for her
death, Edgardo stabs himself, hoping they can be together
at last.

WHAT'S MORE . . .

Lucia di Lammermoor was based on Sir Walter Scott's novel, *The Bride of Lammermoor*, which, in turn, was based on a true story. The "real life" heroine lived in the 17th century and was named Janet Dalrymple, daughter of Lord Stair. She was engaged to a man named Rutherford, but her family disapproved. Her father forced her into a marriage with one David Dunbar of Baldoon instead, and on their wedding night, Janet apparently went mad and stabbed Dunbar. When she was found the next morning, cowering in the fireplace, she said, simply, "Take up your bonny bridegroom." She died a few weeks later of undisclosed causes; Dunbar survived his stabbing and died 12 years later in a fall from his horse. Donizetti's librettist, Cammarano, stuck close to Scott's novel although he made Edgardo's death far more dramatic. In the opera, he stabs himself after hearing of Lucia's death; in the novel, he sinks in quicksand. This might have been difficult to stage!

TO LISTEN FOR

Act I: Lucia's aria "Regnava nel silenzio - Quando rapito in estasi." Act II: Sextet "Che mi frena in tal momento?" Act III: Lucia's mad scene "Il dolce suono . . ."

GIACOMO PUCCINI

Madama Butterfly

Three Acts: First Performance (in 2 acts)—Rome
(La Scala), 1904.
Libretto by G. Giacosa and L. Illica

WHERE AND WHEN
Nagasaki, early 1900s

WHO'S WHO
Cio-Cio-San, or Madama Butterfly (soprano)
B.F. Pinkerton, U.S. Navy lieutenant (tenor)
Sharpless, U.S. consul (baritone)
The Bonze, Butterfly's uncle (bass)
Suzuki, her maid (mezzo-soprano)

WHAT IT'S ABOUT
A geisha gives up everything for the man who promises her
the world. When that promise proves false, she chooses death
over hopelessness and dishonor.

WHAT'S HAPPENING
In Act I, Pinkerton, about to wed Butterfly, insensitively tells
Sharpless how he looks forward to marrying a "real
American" wife. Butterfly enters, unaware, with her most pre-
cious possessions (including the knife her father used to com-
mit hara-kiri). Just as the wedding ceremony ends, the Bonze
insists that her family reject her for renouncing her faith.
When Act II begins, Pinkerton has been away for three years,
and Butterfly has had his son. She refuses to believe she has
been deserted, until Sharpless comes to convince her. She is
devastated—but then, Pinkerton's ship arrives in the harbor.
In Act III, Butterfly's joy is short-lived. Pinkerton and Kate,
his American wife, have come for the boy, and Butterfly, now
futureless, must give him up. Her only course is suicide—
with her father's knife.

WHAT'S MORE . . .
The opening night of *Madama Butterfly* was one of the greatest
fiascos in the history of opera. The entire second act was bare-

ly audible through the boos, whistles, laughter and cat-calls of the audience. The press disliked it as well. Puccini immediately withdrew it and began revisions. He shortened the first act, omitting much tedious local color in the wedding scene (Butterfly's uncle, Yakuside, was seen to get drunk), and divided the almost 90 minute second act—cripplingly long for an Italian audience—in two. He added a brief but beautiful aria for the tenor ("Addio, fiorito asil") who otherwise was practically silent throughout, and shortened and refocused the Butterfly-Kate Pinkerton scene (it was originally Kate who asks for the child). When the revised version was presented three months later it was a resounding success, although Puccini made further revisions until 1906. Nowadays it is impossible to imagine an operatic world without Puccini's sad geisha; had the composer not persisted, we might have lost her forever.

WHAT TO LISTEN FOR

Act I: Butterfly's entrance "Quanto cielo . . . Ancora un passo or via"; Love duet - "Viene le sera." Act II: Butterfly's aria "Un bel di"; Suzuki-Butterfly duet "Scuoti quella fronda di ciliegio." Act III: Pinkerton's aria "Addio fiorito asil"; Butterfly's death aria "Con onor muore . . . "

Manon Lescaut

Four Acts: First Performance—Turin (Regio), 1893
Libretto by Praga, Oliva, Illica, Giacosa, Ricordi, and
the composer

WHERE AND WHEN

France, second half of the 18th century

WHO'S WHO

Manon Lescaut (soprano)
Chevalier des Grieux, a student (tenor)
Lescaut, Manon's brother (baritone)
Geronte, Manon's wealthy, elderly suitor (bass)

WHAT IT'S ABOUT

A young woman en route to the convent gets waylaid by love.
Her piety quickly transforms into pleasure-seeking, and her
fickleness leads to unhappiness for everyone.

WHAT'S HAPPENING

In Act I, Manon and her brother stop at an inn, awaiting a carriage that will take her on to her convent. She catches the eye of Des Grieux, who learns that old Geronte plans to abduct her. He convinces her to run away with him instead. In Act II, in Paris, Manon has been living with Des Grieux, but she is now ensconced with rich Geronte. She is well-cared-for but bored, and when Des Grieux appears, she begs his forgiveness. As they are about to leave together, Geronte has Manon arrested as a harlot and a thief. Act III, near a harbor: Lescaut and Des Grieux hope to rescue Manon before she is deported to America. They almost succeed, but guards suddenly surround them. The ship's captain takes pity on Des Grieux and allows him to come aboard. Act IV takes the couple to Louisiana, where Manon collapses from illness—and self-reproach. She dies in the arms of Des Grieux.

WHAT'S MORE . . .

"Massenet feels it like a Frenchman, with the powder and the minuets. I shall feel it as an Italian, with desperate passion." So stated Giacomo Puccini by way of explanation when he announced that he would set the subject of Abbé Prévost's novel to music so soon after the enormous success of Massenet's *Manon.* Having hurled the gauntlet, Puccini needed a superb libretto, and the search for a fine librettist was on. First came composer friend (and later, enemy (see entry for *La bohème*) Ruggero Leoncavallo, then the novelist Marco Praga, then the poet Domenico Oliva. Ricordi, the publisher, displeased so far, hired Giuseppe Giacosa, and eventually, Luigi Illica. The five of them never quite turned out a masterpiece, but Puccini's music makes up for any weaknesses in the libretto; indeed, it was his first great success and when the opera was performed in London, George Bernard Shaw wrote that Puccini was "more like the heir to Verdi than any of his rivals."

WHAT TO LISTEN FOR

Act I: Des Grieux' aria "Donna non vidi mai." Act II: Manon's aria "In quelle trine morbide"; Des Grieux-Manon duet "Tu, tu, amore? Tu?" Act III: Des Grieux' scene and finale "No, pazzo son!" Act IV: Manon's aria "Sola, perduta, abbandonata."

RICHARD WAGNER

Die Meistersinger von Nürnberg

Three Acts: First Performance, Munich
(Court Theater), 1868
Libretto by the composer

WHERE AND WHEN
Nuremberg, 16th century

WHO'S WHO
Hans Sachs, a cobbler and poet (baritone)
Eva (soprano)
Pogner, Eva's father (bass)
Walther von Stolzing, Eva's suitor (tenor)
Sixtus Beckmesser, town clerk and Walther's rival (baritone)
Magdalene, Eva's nurse (mezzo-soprano)

WHAT IT'S ABOUT
Walther sees two trials looming between him and his beloved
Eva: he must become a member of the Guild of Mastersingers,
and he must win a song contest. It appears he will succeed at
neither; however, he has the wise Hans Sachs on his side. He
also has Eva's love and a musical talent that cannot be denied.

WHAT'S HAPPENING
In Act I, Walther and Eva fall in love; however, she must wed
the winner of the Mastersinger's song contest. Walter audi-
tions for membership—to the jeers of all except Hans Sachs.
Act II: Walther and Eva try to elope. Magdalene, disguised as
Eva, gets serenaded by Beckmesser, and Sachs critiques the
performance with mocking hammer blows to a shoe he is supposedly repairing. He also prevents the ill-conceived escape of
the lovers (and manages to suppress his own love for Eva).
Act III: the day of the contest. Beckmesser steals Walther's
song (thinking it belongs to Sachs) and performs it so badly
that Walther gets his chance. He wins the contest, the girl,
and membership in the Guild. This last honor is by now a bit-
tersweet one, but he accepts it in the name of German Art.

WHAT'S MORE . . .

The character of Beckmesser, the fussy, traditionalist "marker," was modeled by Wagner after Eduard Hanslick, a leading critic of the time who was known for his conservative views—which included a dislike of Wagner's music. Hanslick believed that music was an end in itself and should be performed and heard as such: it wasn't about anything and certainly wasn't subservient to words. Hanslick could be narrow-minded ("For my heart, music really begins with Mozart and culminates in Beethoven, Schumann and Brahms," he wrote), but he was undeniably an excellent critic. However, his excellence didn't interest Wagner, who saw in the half-Jewish Hanslick everything he fought against—both politically and socially.

WHAT TO LISTEN FOR

Act I: Prelude and opening chorus; Walther's song and ensemble "Am stillen herd."

Act II: Sachs' monologue "Was duftet doch der Flieder"; Beckmesser's serenade (with Sach's comments); ensemble and fugal finale "Jerum! Jerum!"

Act III: Sachs' monologue "Wahn! Wahn!"; Quintet "Die selige Morgentraum-Deutweise . . . Selig, wie die Sonne"; Walther's Prize Song "Morgendlich leuchtend im rosigem Schein."

VINCENZO BELLINI

Norma

Two Acts: First Performance, Milan (La Scala), 1831
Libretto by Felice Romani

WHERE AND WHEN
Gaul, first century BC

WHO'S WHO
Norma, High Priestess of the Druid temple (soprano)
Adalgisa, young priestess and Norma's acolyte (soprano)
Pollione, Roman proconsul in Gaul (tenor)
Oroveso, Norma's father (bass)

WHAT IT'S ABOUT
Only tragedy can result when a woman must choose between
the man she loves and the people (and gods) she serves.
Norma, High Priestess of the Druids, has long ago taken her
Vestal Virgin vows. However, she has also borne two children
to Pollione, the Roman who has captured her heart.

WHAT'S HAPPENING
In Act I, Pollione spies on the Druids as they pray for victory
over their Roman masters. He is also enflamed by desire for
Adalgisa, who has replaced Norma in his affections. Later, in
a scene of revelation, Norma learns about her lover's betrayal,
Adalgisa learns that this same man is the father of Norma's
children, and both women join forces in cursing Pollione. Act
II: Norma thinks she must kill her children, but then offers
them to her rival. Adalgisa refuses and renews her own Vestal
vows, attempting to reunite Norma with Pollione. Instead,
Norma hears that Pollione plans to abduct Adalgisa, and she
arranges for him to be burned as a sacrifice to war. However,
she makes herself the victim in his place, and Pollione, seeing
the nobility of the woman he has rejected, joins her on the
pyre.

WHAT'S MORE . . .
The character of Norma is, by turns, authoritative, pious,
motherly, vengeful, understanding, frightened, warm, rueful,

resigned. The character is as varied as the singers who have interpreted the role: Rosa Ponselle had great smoothness of delivery and richness of sound, Gina Cigna added passion, Zinka Milanov's Verdian dignity was impressive, Joan Sutherland's fluency with fioratura (embellishments) was magical, and Montserrat Caballé's exquisite sound was almost overwhelming. But now, from our vantage point near the end of the 20th century, it is safe to say that one "Norma" stands above all the others—Maria Callas, who sang it more than 80 times, between 1948 and 1965. Only Callas projected all of the character's many traits, and only Callas fulfilled Bellini's prescription for opera: "Through singing [it] must make you weep, shudder, die."

TO LISTEN FOR

Act I: Norma's entrance recitative and aria "Sediziose voci . . . Casta diva"; Norma-Adalgisa duet "O rimembranza"; trio finale "Ma di, l'amato giovane . . . O non tremare . . . Vanne si!" Act II: Norma-Adalgisa duet "Mira o norma"; Norma-Pollione duet "In mia man alfin tu sei"; finale "Qual cor tradisti."

WOLFGANG AMADEUS MOZART

Le nozze di Figaro

(The Marriage of Figaro)

Four Acts: First Performance, Vienna (Burgtheater),
1786
Libretto by Lorenzo da Ponte

WHERE AND WHEN
Near Seville, 1780s

WHO'S WHO
Figaro, servant to Count Almaviva (bass)
Susanna, maid to Countess Almaviva (soprano)
Count Almaviva (baritone)
Countess Almaviva, his wife (soprano)
Cherubino, page to the Countess (male role played by mezzo-soprano or soprano)
Dr. Bartolo (bass)
Marcellina, originally his housekeeper (mezzo-soprano)

WHAT IT'S ABOUT
A Count and Countess carry on a quixotic relationship with each other and their servants. There are plots and subplots galore, most of which are aimed at the roguish Count.

WHAT'S HAPPENING
Act I dawns on the wedding day of Figaro and Susanna. The Count, craving Susanna, wishes he could share in the nuptial delights; Marcellina, craving Figaro, wishes he were marrying her. (And he will have to, if he fails to repay her loan of money.) Cherubino, who craves most of the women, is found hiding in the Countess's bedroom. In Act II, these yearnings continue but are confounded by much hiding, peeping, and uncovering. Act III brings the revelation that Dr. Bartolo and Marcellina are the father and mother of Figaro. They might as well get married, along with their son and Susanna. (And Figaro's debt is forgiven.) In Act IV, Susanna is still determined to foil the Count. She leads him to a rendezvous—where he meets up with his wife, instead. By the final curtain, all is forgiven.

WHAT'S MORE . . .

Beaumarchais, *Figaro*'s author, knew how to start a controversy, and did so whenever he could. In *Figaro*, he presented the public with a not-very-happily-married Count and Countess and a servant smarter and more moral than her master—in other words, a play that was highly critical of the existing social order. Performances of the play were banned in Austria, but it *was* published, and once Mozart read it, he was intrigued; it struck him as just

what he'd been looking for. He and his librettist, Lorenzo da Ponte, worked quickly and furtively (Mozart's letters contain very little information about the opera's composition). Da Ponte toned down many of the original references to French politics, but Mozart's characterizations in music tell us everything we have to know about love, honor and justice. The result was a resounding success: despite, or perhaps, because of the original ban, by the third performance, the Emperor had to proscribe encores (except of arias) for fear that the opera would go on through the night.

WHAT TO LISTEN FOR

Act I: Figaro's arias "Se vuol ballare"and "Non piu andrai."
Act II: Countess's aria "Porgi amor"; Cherubino's arietta "Voi che sapete"; Finale "Esci, omai, etc . . . " Act III: Count's recitative and aria "Hai gia vinta la causa . . . Vedro Mentr'io sospiro"; Sextet "Riconosci in questo amplesso"; Countess's aria "Dove sono." Act IV: Figaro's aria "Aprite un po' quegli occhi"; Susanna's aria "Deh, vieni, non tardar."

CHRISTOPH WILLABALD GLUCK

Orfeo ed Euridice

Three Acts: First performance—Vienna (Burgtheater), 1762
Text by Raniero de Calzabigi

WHERE AND WHEN
Greece, mythological time

WHO'S WHO
Orfeo, a musician (contralto or tenor)
Euridice, his dead wife (soprano)
Amor, God of Love (soprano)

WHAT IT'S ABOUT
As in the classical myth of Orpheus and Euridice, Orfeo gets his chance to rescue his wife from the Underworld. Also as in the myth, there is a hitch (don't look back) that becomes an impossible feat. However, the power of music is great, and operates here as the spark that fires the *deus ex machina*.

WHAT'S HAPPENING

Act I reveals Orfeo grieving by Euridice's tomb. Just as he makes up his mind to follow her fate, Amor, the God of Love, brings good news from Jupiter. Orfeo may descend in search of his wife, and if he plays his lyre pleasingly enough, he may bring her back with him. However: he must not gaze upon her until they return. In Act II, Orfeo runs the gauntlet of the Furies and placates them with song. He sings again as the Happy Shades approach, and they present him with Euridice. He takes her hand, overjoyed, but he is careful not to look at her face. Act III. Orfeo and Euridice begin their journey back into the world. She can't understand what seems to be his coldness and threatens to return to Hades if he will not look upon her. He can only comply, and, when he does, she dies. Orfeo prepares to kill himself by singing a lament. It is so moving that Amor intervenes, restoring Euridice to life and to her long-suffering husband.

WHAT'S MORE . . .

When Gluck set out to "reform" opera, he did so with a vengeance. The traditions of *opera seria*, filled with subplots, disguises and confused machinations, went against "good sense and reason," he claimed with some justification, and with *Orfeo ed Eurydice*, he set out to alter them . . . Gone were the singers' meaningless showpieces, gone the arias filled with brain-twisting metaphors, gone the endless volley of melodies which had little or nothing to do with the text being sung. *Orfeo*'s plot is simple and direct; the melodies, too, are simple and direct. The emotions are straightforward and natural. Dance and choral movements are fully integrated, not meaningless diversions. Of course, not all was natural: the role of Orfeo was composed for a castrato. But even this was later "reformed." In 1774 when Gluck reworked the opera for Paris, he rewrote it for tenor.

WHAT TO LISTEN FOR

Act I: Orfeo's aria "Chiamo il mio ben cosi." Act II: Orfeo's aria "Che puro ciel." Act III: Orfeo's aria "Che faro senza Eurydice?"

GIUSEPPE VERDI

Otello

Four Acts: First Performance, Milan (La Scala), 1887
Libretto by Arrigo Boito

WHERE AND WHEN
Cyprus, late 15th century

WHO'S WHO
Otello the Moor, governor of Cyprus and general in Venetian army (tenor)
Desdemona, his wife (soprano)
Iago, Otello's ensign (baritone)
Emilia, his wife and Desdemona's lady-in-waiting (mezzo-soprano)
Cassio, Otello's lieutenant (tenor)
Roderigo, young nobleman (tenor)

WHAT IT'S ABOUT
Verdi's *Otello* is a distillation of Shakepeare's tragedy about the devastations of jealousy. Iago's jealousy translates into evil cunning; Otello's plays itself out in a murderous fury. Although both men are responsible for Desdemona's death, Otello has acted out of misplaced trust and a surfeit of passion. Iago's actions are malignity in search of a motive.

WHAT'S HAPPENING
Act I: Among the crowd waiting for the return of the victorious general are the scheming Iago and Roderigo. Iago despises Otello for promoting Cassio to a higher rank, and Roderigo wants Otello's wife for himself. Later, Iago contrives a fight between Roderigo and Cassio, causing Otello to rescind Cassio's post. Act II: Iago, however, is not satisfied; he thickens his evil plot. He convinces Cassio to engage Desdemona's aid in restoring his command; then, bringing Otello to the scene, succeeds in arousing in him the most evil suspicions. Act III: Iago plants Desdemona's handkerchief on Cassio. Otello recognizes it as belonging to his wife, and, in Act IV, he murders her. Then, too late, Emilia and Cassio produce

evidence of Desdemona's innocence, and, as Iago flees the scene, Otello needs to hear no more. He stabs himself.

WHAT'S MORE . . .

The contribution of Arrigo Boito, *Otello*'s librettist, is, arguably, almost as great as Verdi's to the success of the opera. Boito's version is about one-quarter the length of Shakespeare's, but nothing is lost. By eliminating Shakespeare's first act entirely, the action begins and ends in Cyprus; Desdemona's father, the Duke, and Brabantio are eliminated; and the opera can begin in the middle of a storm, creating what is assuredly one of the most stunning opening tableaux in all of opera. What was needed from Act I— some Rodrigo-Iago dialogue to clarify motivation, Otello's and Desdemona's remembrances of their courtship—are very effectively woven in, with the latter becoming part of Verdi's most beautiful love duet. And when Boito invented lines, such as Otello's 12-bar entrance, which establishes him as a great hero (as well as a great tenor!) and Iago's evil-personified "Credo," the invention is brilliant. The Boito-Verdi collaboration remains, along with those of da Ponte-Mozart and Hoffmansthal-Strauss, one of the most profitable in operatic history.

WHAT TO LISTEN FOR

Act I: Iago's drinking song "Inaffia l'ugola"; Otello-Desdemona duet "Gia nella notte densa." Act II: Iago's "Credo"; Otello's aria "Ora e per sempre, addio"; Otello-Iago duet "Si, pel ciel." Act III: Otello-Desdemona duet "Dio to giocondi"; ensemble finale "A terra, si . . . nel livido fango." Act IV: Desdemona's Willow Song and Ave Maria; Otello's final scene "Niun mi tema."

RUGGERO LEONCAVALLO

Pagliaccci

Prologue and Two Acts: First Performance, Milan (dal Verme), 1892
Libretto by the composer, inspired by a court case judged by his father

WHERE AND WHEN
Calabrian village, 19th century

WHO'S WHO
Canio, head of a troupe of strolling players (tenor)
> (In the play, he is Pagliaccio)

Nedda, his wife (soprano)
> (In the play, she is Colombina)

Tonio, a member of the troupe (baritone)
> (In the play, Taddeo)

Silvio, a villager (baritone)

WHAT IT'S ABOUT
A play within a play, showing how fantasy and reality can merge, and how simple farce can become tragic drama.

WHAT'S HAPPENING

The Prologue presents Tonio (Taddeo), who warns the opera audience that the passions to come may not be limited to the actors' stage. In Act I, the villagers welcome the players and spirits are high all around—even though Canio warns that to joke about infidelity on stage is one thing; real-life cuckoldry is quite another. Later, Tonio flirts with Nedda, but she taunts and curses him and strikes him with a whip. Nedda is also unhappy with her husband and arranges a rendezvous with Silvio. Overhearing, the bitter Tonio tells Canio, but the show must go on. In Act II, the play is performed. Nedda takes the role of an unfaithful lover, the demented Canio stabs both her and Silvio, and then, near hysteria, he tells the audience: "The comedy is over."

WHAT'S MORE . . .

Stylistically speaking, Ruggero Leoncavallo did one of the sharpest turnarounds in opera. He was writing a trilogy of operas based in Renaissance Italy called *Crepusculum* when Mascagni's *Cavalleria Rusticana* was successfully premiered. This sent Leoncavallo over the compositional edge, so to speak, and he abandoned the ranks of the classicists and post-Wagnerians and became a leading exponent of *verismo* operas, those "slices of life" about real people in unidealized situations. His *Pagliacci* is the ideal *verismo* opera: The fourth wall is broken immediately when Tonio addresses the audience in his "prologue"; there are anger, adultery, rage and revenge galore, and a character is killed in full view of the audience. And when Canio tells the audience at the opera's close that "la commedia è finito," all theatrical politeness is abandoned— we have become a party to a crime.

WHAT TO LISTEN FOR

Act I: Prologue, sung by Tonio, the clown; Canio's scena "Un tal gioco"; Canio's aria "Vesti la giubba." Act II: Pagliacci's outburst and finale "No, Pagliacco non son."

BENJAMIN BRITTEN

Peter Grimes

Prologue, Three Acts, Epilogue: First Performance—
Sadler's Wells), 1945
Libretto by Montague Slater

WHERE AND WHEN
Fishing village(the Borough), east coast of England,
around 1830

WHO'S WHO
Peter Grimes, a fisherman (tenor)
Ellen Orford, schoolmistress (soprano)
Captain Balstrode, retired skipper (baritone)

WHAT IT'S ABOUT
The villagers suspect Peter Grimes of causing his first apprentice's death, and his reclusive behavior does nothing to change
their opinion. However, one woman, the widow Ellen Orford,
espouses Grime's cause. Together with the kindly Captain
Balstrode, she almost changes Grimes's destiny, but he is too
much of an outcast and too much a victim of his own tortured mind to be saved . . . and more death will follow.

WHAT'S HAPPENING
The Prologue opens with the inquest of the apprentice's death
at sea. Grimes is officially cleared, but warned that, as a harsh
taskmaster, he should employ grown men instead of youths.
Ellen Orford raises her voice of support for Grimes against
the villagers' outrage. Act I reveals life in the village, under-
scoring Grimes's isolation from it. When Ellen appears with
his new apprentice, a lad from the workhouse, Grimes shows
immediately that he is still a hard master, and, in Act II,
Ellen's own suspicions are aroused when she sees on the boy
marks of a beating. She tries to intervene, but in vain—
Grimes drives the youth to exhaustion, and accidentally causes
his death. By Act III, the boy's disappearance causes height-
ened speculation and censure; even Ellen and Balstrode have
their doubts. In the Epilogue, the two come across the now-
demented Grimes on the beach, and Balstrode advises him to

take himself back out to sea, and to sink his boat. Word comes to the village that a ship has gone down, but curiosity has dwindled, and life goes on as usual.

WHAT'S MORE . . .

In *Peter Grimes*, Britten has created one of the most formidable villains in all of opera. No, it isn't the outcast, the somewhat dangerous and occasionally violent title character; one gets the feeling that he could, under different circumstances, be rehabilitated. It is, rather, the populace of the village in which the opera is set. Britten's gift for individual characterization was never more vivid than it is here: the troublemaking, hypocritical Mrs Sedley, the quack/apothecary Ned Keene, the bullying, drunken, self-righteous Bob Boles. But it is as a group—a mob, really (only Ellen and Captain Balstrode offer humanity)—that the inhabitants of the Borough become truly dangerous. They hate Grimes's "differentness" and they literally hound him to insanity. Britten's obvious identification with Grimes makes the opera work: he and his companion, Peter Pears, were homosexuals and pacifists—in their own words, they were "individuals against the crowd." And so, in his own way, is Peter Grimes.

TO LISTEN FOR

Act I: Ellen's aria "Let her among you without sin cast the first stone"; Peter's scene "Now the Great Bear and Pleiades." Act II: Ellen-chorus-Peter "This unrelenting work"; Scene 2: Peter "Go there . . . In dreams I've built myself some kindlier home." Act III: Ellen's aria "Embroidery in childhood was a luxury of idleness"; Peter's mad scene "Steady. There you are. Nearly home."

GIUSEPPE VERDI

Rigoletto

Three Acts: First Performance—Venice
(La Fenice), 1851

WHERE AND WHEN
16th century Italy

WHO'S WHO
The Duke of Mantua (tenor)
Rigoletto, the Duke's jester (baritone)
Gilda, Rigoletto's daughter (soprano)
Monterone, a nobleman (baritone)
Sparafucile, an assassin (bass)
Maddalena, his sister (contralto)

WHAT IT'S ABOUT
Rigoletto's role as court jester suits his embittered existence.
He is a deformed man—a hunchback—and alone except for
his daughter Gilda, whom he is determined to shelter from the
cruel caprices of life at court. Rigoletto's obsessive fatherly
devotion leads indirectly to what he fears the most, and this
irony catapults the story to its tragic end.

WHAT'S HAPPENING
In Act I, Rigoletto lauds the lechery of the Duke of Mantua,
and is cursed by Count Monterone, whose daughter has been
the Duke's most recent victim. Rigoletto does not know that
the Duke has also flirted with his beloved Gilda and won her
heart. The scheming courtiers kidnap Gilda, tricking
Rigoletto into helping by pretending she is someone else, and
they carry her off to the Duke. In Act II, Rigoletto realizes
what has happened and swears revenge. Act III: seeing that
Gilda has fallen in love with her seducer, he arranges for
Sparafucile to murder the Duke. However, Maddalena convinces her brother to substitute another victim. Gilda, overhearing and determined to save her lover, volunteers. Because
she is in disguise, Rigoletto unwittingly orders his daughter's
murder. The curse—*la maledizione*—has been fulfilled.

WHAT'S MORE . . .

Details surrounding the creation of *Rigoletto* were, as usual, complicated. The censors wanted to eliminate Monterone cursing the Duke because royalty mustn't be cursed; they didn't like the sack in which Sparafucile delivers Gilda to Rigoletto near the opera's end; and they didn't want Rigoletto to be a hunchback. Verdi won on all three counts, and the public followed all of the intrigue. But just days before the supposed premiere, a question was still being asked: was there to be a tenor aria in the last act? No one had heard or seen it—not even the orchestra and the tenor. Verdi was careful to keep it from them; he knew that once it was heard, it would catch on so quickly that by the time it was actually heard in performance, people would think that he had stolen it! And so it was only during the final rehearsal that cast and orchestra got to hear "La donna e mobile," and the day after the premiere, everyone in Venice knew it—the aria became the popular song of the season.

TO LISTEN FOR

Act I: Rigoletto's "Pari siamo; " Gilda's "Caro nome."
Act II: Rigoletto's aria "Cortigiani, vil razza, dannata";
Rigoletto-Gilda duet "Tutte le feste al tempio."
Act III: The duke's "La donna e mobile"; quartet "Bella figlia dell'amore."

RICHARD WAGNER

Der Ring des Nibelungen

A Prelude and Three Operas, First Complete
Performance—Bayreuth, August 1876
Libretto by the composer

WHERE AND WHEN
In and about the River Rhine, legendary time

WHAT IT'S ABOUT
The *Ring* cycle consists of *Das Rheingold* (The Rhinegold), *Die Walküre* (The Valkyrie), *Siegfried*, and *Götterdämmerung* (Twilight of the Gods). The story begins with the theft of the most powerful gold conceivable: whoever makes a ring out of it while at the same time denouncing love will be ruler of the world. Unfortunately for the characters, by the end of the story—the final curtain of the fourth opera—there's nothing much left to rule. Fortunately for the audience, up to that point, there has been just about everything: giants and dwarves, marriages and murders, a little bit of incest and a whole lot of greed. No mere slice of life is Wagner's *Ring*; it's an epic chunk for hearty appetites.

. . . .

Das Rheingold

WHO'S WHO
The Rhinemaidens (two sopranos and a mezzo-soprano)
Alberich, the Nibelung dwarf (baritone)
Wotan, chief of the gods (baritone)
Fricka, his wife, goddess of marriage (mezzo-soprano)
Loge, god of fire (tenor)
Fasolt and **Fafner**, giants/castle-builders (basses)
Freia, goddess of love, Fricka's sister (soprano)
Erda, earth goddess (contralto)

WHAT'S HAPPENING
The Rhinemaidens are guardians of the magical gold. The dwarf Alberich steals the treasure and makes a ring—*the* Ring, following the instructions to renounce love at the same time. He's all set to rule the world, but the god Wotan usurps the

Ring, and Alberich puts a curse on it, to wreak destruction
upon whoever possesses it. Unaware of this drawback, Wotan
will use the Ring to reclaim Freia, without whose golden
apples the gods cannot remain immortal. Wotan had previously traded Freia to Fasolt and Fafner for their construction
of his castle, Valhalla, and Erda underscores the folly of this
action by predicting the downfall of the gods. As soon as the
giants are in possession of the Ring, Fafner kills Fasolt. The
curse has begun its work, even as the gods take up residency in
the magnificent Valhalla.

WHAT TO LISTEN FOR
Opening scene: in the Rhine with Alberich and the
Rhinemaidens; the god Donner's call to the clouds - "Heda,
heda, hedo"; and the Entry of the Gods into Valhalla.

....

Die Walküre

WHO'S WHO
(in addition to some of the characters from *Das Rheingold*):
Siegmund, mortal son of Wotan (tenor)
Sieglinde, mortal daughter of Wotan (soprano)
Brünnhilde (soprano) and eight other Valkyries, daughters of
Wotan and Erda (sopranos, etc.)
Hunding, husband to Sieglinde (bass)

WHAT'S HAPPENING
Sieglinde and Siegmund, mortal twins born to Wotan, reunite
as adults when a storm drives him to seek shelter in her hut.
Sieglinde has been living there with Hunding, the man to

whom she is unhappily married, and who is also the enemy of Siegmund. The twins soon fall in love and flee together, taking with them "Nothung," the sword once belonging to their father. Wotan is also father to the nine Valkyries, and he orders his favorite, Brünnhilde, to side with Hunding during his duel with Siegmund. Brünnhilde, sympathetic to her mortal siblings, crosses her father and promises victory to Siegmund. However, urged on by Fricka (who guards the sanctity of marriage) Wotan appears, shatters the sword, and presides over his own son's death. Brünnhilde rescues the shattered pieces of Nothung; she also rescues Sieglinde, who is carrying Siegmund's child. Wotan must punish Brünnhilde for this act of disobedience, so he leaves her to sleep surrounded by fire; however, since he also loves her so dearly, he declares that when she is rescued, it must be by a great hero.

WHAT TO LISTEN FOR

Act I: Siegmund-Sieglinde duet beginning with "Der Männer sippe" to the end of the act. Act II: Brünnhilde's Battle Cry "Hojotojo!"; Brünnhilde-Siegmund "announcement of death" scene. Act III: Ride of the Valkyries; Magic Fire Music.

....

Siegfried

WHO'S WHO

(In addition to some of the characters already introduced):
Siegfried, son of Siegmund and Sieglinde (tenor)
Mime, Alberich's brother (tenor)
Forest Bird (soprano)

WHAT'S HAPPENING

Sieglinde has died giving birth to her brother's child,
Siegfried, who was found and raised by Mime. Siegfried, now
a man, seeks to reclaim the Ring by slaying Fafner, who lives
in a cave nearby, having taken on the form of a dragon.
Siegfried succeeds in reforging the only instrument worthy of
such a task—Nothung—the sword that been wielded by his
father and by Wotan before him. Siegfried kills Fafner and
drinks some dragon blood, thus gaining the ability to understand the instructions of the Forest Bird. These chirpings lead
him toward the spot where Brünnhilde lies inside her circle of
fire. Wotan tries to stop him, but Siegfried wins out, not
knowing his opponent's identity. As he destroys Wotan's
spear, rulership passes from god to man. Siegfried then claims
Brünnhilde, who is at first horrified at the thought of surrender; however, she can't resist the forces of love.

WHAT TO LISTEN FOR

Act I: Siegfried's Forging Song "Nothung! Nothung!" Act
II: Forest Murmurs; Siegfried-Dragon fight. Act III:
Brünnhilde's awakening and final scene "Heil dir, Sonne!"

Götterdämmerung

WHO'S WHO

(In addition to some of the characters already introduced):
Gunther, a male Gibichung (baritone)
Gutrune, a female Gibichung (soprano)
Hagen, their half-brother (bass)
Waltraute, Brünnhilde's sister (mezzo-soprano)

WHAT'S HAPPENING

Hagen, son of Alberich, sets out to recapture the Ring, which
is now on Brünnhilde's finger. He plots with the Gibichungs
Gunther and Gutrune, and they give Siegfried a drug that

destroys his memory, making him think he loves Gutrune and that he must deliver Brünnhilde to Gunther. In disguise, and still duped by the drug, Siegfried takes the Ring from Brünnhilde, places it on his own finger, and allows his wife to think he loves another woman. During the confusion that follows, Hagen kills Siegfried, but when he tries to take from his victim the Ring, Brünnhilde intercedes. Having discovered, too late, that Siegfried was not responsible for his actions, she orders a huge funeral pyre and joins Siegfried in death. Brünnhilde's sacrifice—out of sorrow and love and despair—creates a maelstrom. The Rhine overflows; the Rhinemaidens appear to reclaim the Ring—now cleansed of its curse; and the funeral fire spreads to Valhalla. The power of the gods has ended. A new era begins.

TO LISTEN FOR

Prologue: Siegfried and Brünnhilde's duet and Siegfried's Rhine Journey. Act I: Hagen's Watch. Act II: Siegfried-Brünnhilde confrontation "Helle wehr! Heilige Götter!" Act III: Siegfried's death and Funeral Music; Brünnhilde's Immolation Scene.

WHAT'S MORE . . .

In the *Ring*, which took 28 years to complete, Wagner's goal was to create a work (or series of works—"tetralogy" was the word he used; he further described it as "A stage festival play for three days and a preliminary evening") would realize his theory of *Gesamtkunstwerk*, a unity of words, music and stage action designed to intermingle perfectly, each playing an equal role. And, since he considered himself a brilliant playwright, philosopher, stage director and poet as well as composer, who better than he to concoct such perfection?

Well, in the *Ring*, as in his other operas, the poetry is often turgid and the drama is frequently outlandish and static ("Wagner has some wonderful moments," wrote a critic many years ago, "and some terrible half-hours") and his great hero, Siegfried, tends, at times, to be no more than a callow, insensitive, stupid lout.

But *Gesamtkunstwerk* or not, Wagner has created an amazing parable of humanity that deals with love, lust, loyalty, and the thirst for and corruption of power on a most human level. We genuinely care about Wotan, the guilty, loving, vain god who watches his power slip away, at times gladly, at times ruefully; Brünnhilde, the energetic warrior who is also a complete, passionate woman; Siegmund and Sieglinde, torn apart by, and then brought together by fate; Fricka, who can never forgive

her husband his infidelities, and many others—even the hateful Hagen, Alberich and Mime manage to keep us spellbound.

And whatever criticisms one may make of the drama and its *longueurs*, the music remains above it all and larger than life: never before or since have so many feelings been expressed so vividly and viscerally in one work. Like it or not, it is the pinnacle.

RICHARD STRAUSS

Der Rosenkavalier

(The Cavalier of the Rose)

Three Acts: First Performance, Dresden, 1911
Libretto by Hugo von Hofmannsthal

WHERE AND WHEN
Vienna, mid-18th century

WHO'S WHO
The Marschallin, or Princess von Werdenberg (soprano)
Baron Ochs, her cousin (bass)
Octavian, the Marschallin's young lover (male role played by
mezzo-soprano)
Herr von Faninal (baritone)
Sophie, his daughter (soprano)

WHAT IT'S ABOUT
A young man wins his new love by a scheme wherein he mas-
querades as a chambermaid. Meanwhile, his old love faces the
mirror and the truth: she must surrender her seductive power
to a younger and prettier woman.

WHAT'S HAPPENING
In Act I, Octavian is *en flagrant* with the married Marschallin
when the loutish Baron Ochs barges in. Octavian disguises
himself as a chambermaid, and Ochs is enticed. However,
Ochs is engaged to Sophie, and he has really come in search of
a cavalier to present to her the traditional silver rose. The
Marschallin offers Octavian's services, and in Act II, Sophie
and Octavian meet and fall instantly in love. She is naturally
now even more appalled to meet Ochs: her future groom. To
save the young beauty, Octavian duels with Ochs, whose slight
wounds are healed by the promise of a second meeting with
the luscious "maid." As Act III unfolds, Octavian exposes
Ochs's roguery to Sophie's father and breaks the marriage
contract. Now Octavian must face the Marschallin. She has
known this would one day happen, so she sends her lover into
the younger woman's arms.

WHAT'S MORE . . .

In both *Salome* and *Elektra*, Strauss had examined perverse female obsessions, hysterical dancing and hideous deaths; with his next opera, *Der Rosenkavalier*, he continued his fascination with women and the female voice but did a 180-degree turn emotionally and psychologically. In *Rosenkavalier*, Strauss features three star female voices (although one character, Octavian is a *travesti* role—Strauss's answer to Mozart's Cherubino, he claimed). However, the vocal lines soar gracefully rather than violently, and in place of the anguish of the two earlier operas, we are given nostalgia, generosity, humor, and a smile towards the future. And what of the frenzied dancing? Strauss has replaced it with waltzes worthy of that other Strauss, Johann.

WHAT TO LISTEN FOR

Act I: Marschallin's monologue "Da geht er hin . . . "
Act II: Presentation of the Silver Rose "Mir ist die Ehre widerfahren"; Ochs' waltz song "Ohne mich, ohne mich."
Act II: Trio "Marie Theres'!"

RICHARD STRAUSS

Salome

One Act: First Performance, Dresden
(Court Opera), 1905
Libretto adapted by the composer

WHERE AND WHEN
Galilee, c. 30 AD

WHO'S WHO
Salome, Princess of Judea (soprano)
Jochanaan, or John the Baptist (bass-baritone)
Herod, King of Judea (tenor)
Herodias, Salome's mother (mezzo-soprano)
Narraboth, a slave (tenor)

WHAT IT'S ABOUT

The New Testament story of Salome could well be subtitled *Hell hath no fury like a woman scorned*. The scorner is Jochanaan (John the Baptist), whose piety makes him morally immune to the beautiful sinner's charms.

WHAT'S HAPPENING

Salome, stepdaughter of Herod, becomes entranced by the voice of Jochanaan, prophesying from his dungeon. She seduces the guard and gets him to bring the prisoner up to her. Jochanaan denounces Salome's mother, the Queen, for killing her husband in order to marry Herod, and he rejects Salome's every advance. Even so, her lust for him only grows, driving her nearly insane. She pretends to accept the advances of her stepfather, Herod, and he promises her anything in return for a dance. She performs the Dance of the Seven Veils and then demands John the Baptist's head. Herod reluctantly complies, and she revels in her prize, kissing the severed head as her mother laughs her approval. Herod, sickened by the scene, orders her crushed to death by his soldiers.

WHAT'S MORE . . .

After the public and critical disapproval of both *Guntram* and *Feuersnot*, Strauss began to be seen as a rebel. A journal entry reads "It's unbelievable what enemies *Guntram* has made . . . I shall shortly be put on trial as a dangerous criminal." Of course, Strauss was exaggerating, but with his next opera, *Salome*, his reputation as a scandal-maker was assured. The opera was called blasphemous. The Metropolitan in New York presented it for one night and then withdrew it, with the press stating that "*Salome* is a detailed and explicit exposition of the most horrible, disgusting, revolting and unmentionable features of degeneracy that I have ever heard of, read of, or imagined . . . Strauss's music is aesthetically criminal." The upshot of the controversy? There were productions of *Salome* in 50 different opera houses within the next two years!

WHAT TO LISTEN FOR

Jochanaan-Salome scene "Wo ist er . . . "
Salome's Dance of the Seven Veils
Final scene "Ah, du wolltest mich nicht deinen Mund küssen lassen."

CAMILLE SAINT-SAËNS

Samson et Dalila

Three Acts: First Performance—Weimer
(Hoftheater), 1877
Libretto by Ferdinand Lemaire

WHERE AND WHEN
Gaza (Palestine), B.C.

WHO'S WHO
Dalila, a Philistine (mezzo-soprano)
Samson, leader of the Hebrews (tenor)
High Priest (baritone)

WHAT IT'S ABOUT
Following her Old Testament (Book of Judges) counterpart,
Saint-Saëns' Dalila uncovers the source of Samson's superhu-
man strength and brings about his defeat at the hands of her
fellow Philistines.

WHAT'S HAPPENING
In Act I, Samson leads his people to victory against their
oppressors, slaying the Satrap of Gaza and scattering the
Philistines into the hills. Among the defeated is Dalila, who
returns to congratulate her conqueror and former lover.
Samson, in spite of himself, is again mesmerized by her
charms and, in Act II, appears at her house. Although he has
planned to tell her farewell, she wins out and entraps him.
Overcome by passion, Samson reveals that his hair holds the
secret of his power, and Dalila is triumphant. Act III: Samson,
shorn (and blinded for good measure), lies in a dungeon. He
endures the taunts of Dalila, his captors, his own people, and,
most of all, his conscience. Later, as the scornful revelry reach-
es fever pitch, he regains enough strength to pull down the
temple on the heads of all.

WHAT'S MORE . . .

The libretto for *Samson et Dalila* was written by an in-law of the composer's, based on Chapter 16 of the Book of Judges. However, rather than depict the epic sections of the chapter, such as Samson's winning duel with a lion or his slaying of a thousand Philistines with the jawbone of an ass, Lemaire and Saint-Saëns concentrated on the character of Dalila. This arch seductress manipulates the plot with her intensity (and her beautiful melodies); her motivations are less political than sensual. One can say the same for Samson; in fact, these two are a perfectly matched couple, except for the fact that she decides to destroy him. And so the Biblical background becomes just that—background—and what Saint-Saëns and his librettist offer us is an exquisitely perverse love story with a tragic ending, full of atmosphere.

WHAT TO LISTEN FOR

Act I: Samson and chorus "Arretez, mes frères!"; Dalila's aria "Printemps qui commence." Act II: Samson-Dalila scene "En ces lieux, malgré moi . . . Mon coeur s'ouvre a ta voix." Act III: Samson's scene "Vois ma misère, hélas!"; Bacchanale.

GIACOMO PUCCINI

Tosca

Three Acts: First Performance—Rome
(Teatro Constanzi), 1900
L. Illica and G. Giacosa

WHERE AND WHEN
Rome, 1800

WHO'S WHO
Mario Cavaradossi, a painter (tenor)
Floria Tosca, a singer (soprano)
Scarpia, the chief of police (baritone)
Angelotti, a political prisoner (bass)

WHAT IT'S ABOUT
Tosca is a singer—a prima donna whose passions run high,
especially for her lover, the high-minded Cavaradossi. Her
tempestuous nature makes her an easy mark for the diabolical
Scarpia, whose heart is as cold as hers is hot. The outcome
teeters on the brink of happiness; alas, tragedy befalls.

WHAT'S HAPPENING
Act I opens in the Church of Sant'Andrea della Valle, where
Mario Cavaradossi is painting a mural. When Angelotti dash-
es onto the scene, Cavaradossi offers to hide him in his well.
Tosca makes her entrance, misinterpreting her lover's secrecy
for an intrigue with Angelotti's sister. Scarpia feeds her suspicions. He hopes for information and, eventually, for Tosca
herself. In Act II, Scarpia arrests Cavaradossi, even though the
police have found no evidence of his treason. Tosca appears,
and Cavaradossi tells her the truth before he is taken away to
be tortured. Forced to listen to her lover's screams, Tosca
breaks down and tells Scarpia all he needs for a conviction.
After Scarpia sends Cavaradossi off to await execution, he
offers to arrange a mock firing squad in exchange for Tosca's
favors. She agrees, but, as soon as he has written out the
orders, she stabs him. Act III reveals Cavaradossi in jail, brave-
ly facing his fate. Tosca rushes in and tells him that the execution will be only a pretense. With a happy heart, he takes his

place atop the castle, but the firing squad means business after all. Scarpia's evil has lived on after him, and Tosca leaps off the parapet, following Cavaradossi in death.

WHAT'S MORE . . .

Tosca has been called "a shabby little shocker," and, indeed, the opera's realism is gritty and cold-blooded enough to make responsible parents keep their children at home. But it is musically realistic as well—Puccini made certain of that. For the *Te Deum* which closes the first act, for instance, the composer consulted a priest about the correct plainsong melody. Further, a musician in the Vatican informed him of the exact pitch of the bell of St. Peter's, and the words to the Roman shepherd boy's Act III song were specifically written by a Roman poet. Finally, Puccini himself went to Rome to hear what the matin bells sounded like from the top of the Castel Sant'Angelo, where the opera's third act is set. In other words, *Tosca* may be shocking, but its composition was anything but shabby— it evokes Rome and the church as well as individual passions.

TO LISTEN FOR:

Act I:
Cavaradossi's aria
"Recondite armonia";
Scarpia and chorus *Te Deum*. Act II: Tosca's aria "Vissi d'arte."
Act III:
Cavaradossi's aria
"E lucevan le stelle."

GIUSEPPE VERDI

La Traviata

(The Lost One)

Three Acts: First Performance—Venice
(La Fenice), 1853
Libretto by Francesco Maria Piave

WHERE AND WHEN

Paris and the French countryside, 1850

WHO'S WHO

Violetta Valery, a courtesan (soprano)
Alfredo Germont, her lover (tenor)
Giorgio Germont, his father (baritone)
Baron Douphol, Alfredo's rival (baritone)

WHAT IT'S ABOUT

Violetta is the ultimate sympathetic character. She is a saint in
courtesan's clothing, who gives up her happiness and even her
life to do right (what she thinks is right) by the man she loves.

WHAT'S HAPPENING

Act I includes the famous Parisian party scene, during which
Violetta and Alfredo meet and fall in love. In Act II, Violetta
has renounced her fancy living and has settled in the countryside with young Germont. His wealthy family disapproves, so
Violetta secretly sells her jewels to support their ménage. The
elder Germont pleads with Violetta to give up Alfredo for the
sake of family honor. Even though she knows that she suffers
from consumption, and that leaving Alfredo will only make
her worse, she returns to Paris and takes up with Douphol.
Unaware of her true motives, Alfredo appears at a soireé,
denounces her, and challenges his rival to a duel. By Act III,
we return to Violetta's chambers, where she lies dying.
Germont Père relents and tells his son of her unselfishness.
The lovers reunite, but only briefly—Violetta dies in
Alfredo's arms.

The London Times, August 11, 1856: "An unfortunate young person who has acted the part of a public prostitute . . . coughs her way through three acts and finally expires . . . in a manner which . . . ought to be revolting to the feelings of the spectators."

The outrage was almost universal. Verdi had dared to compose an opera based on a work by Alexandre Dumas *fils*, based on the life of the author's former lover, Alphonsine Plessis, an exquisite courtesan who had died of consumption a mere six years before the opera was produced. Plessis, make no mistake, was not the near-saintly sacrificer of novel, play and opera—"lying makes my teeth white" she was quoted as saying. However, the Romanticism of the age glorified her to poets and composers while she remained horrifying to the general public. As a result of the facts—not the fictions—the opera's premiere was a catastrophe. The furor died down eventually and the glorious fiction and more glorious music remained; *Traviata* is one of the most beloved operas in the repertoire.

TO LISTEN FOR

Act I: Violetta's double aria "Ah, forse lui . . . Sempre libera."
Act II: the Violetta-Germont duet "Dite alle giovane." Act
III: Violetta's aria "Addio del passato"; the Violetta-Alfredo
duet "Parigi, o cara."

GIUSEPPE VERDI

Il trovatore

(The Troubadour)

Four Acts: First Performance, Rome
(Teatro Apollo), 1853
Libretto by Salvatore Cammarano

WHERE AND WHEN
Spain, 15th century

WHO'S WHO
Leonora, a lady-in-waiting (soprano)
Azucena, a gypsy (mezzo-soprano)
Manrico, a troubadour (tenor)
Count di Luna (baritone)
Ferrando, a captain of the guard (bass)

WHAT IT'S ABOUT
Count di Luna and Manrico are on opposite sides in a civil
war; they are also rivals for the hand of Leonora. The enemies
do not discover in time that they are, in fact, brothers, an
irony that might have changed the course of all events.

WHAT'S HAPPENING

In Act I, Ferrando tells how the Count's brother was stolen in infancy and murdered by a vengeful gypsy. When a mysterious troubadour, Manrico, appears, no one knows that he is the missing brother. Leonora falls in love with him, and the Count challenges him to a duel. In Act II, Azucena tells that she was the gypsy who took Manrico away and raised him as her own. Meanwhile, Leonora, believing Manrico to be dead, prepares to enter a convent. The Count plans to abduct her, but Manrico saves her just in time. Act III brings the capture of Azucena, and, in trying to free her, Manrico is himself taken prisoner. Act IV: Leonora pleads with the Count to take her and let Manrico go. She poisons herself, the Count executes Manrico, and only then does Azucena reveal her long-kept secret.

WHAT'S MORE . . .

The plot of *Il trovatore* has so often been parodied and so often deemed incomprehensible that one forgets how many great stage works are remembered for the effects they have on their audience rather than for the niceties of their plots. And there's hardly an opera lover who isn't affected by *Il trovatore*. Some are taken by the poetry to be found in its nighttime settings and private, introspective moments. Others concern themselves with its spookiness: late-night campfire stories about kidnapped, burned babies, or the crazed, witch-like character of Azucena. And others appreciate the medieval world it evokes, with its combination of chivalry, heroics and violence. But everyone agrees that the music is unstoppably stunning. "It is easy to perform *Il trovatore*," said Enrico Caruso. "All you need are the four greatest singers in the world."

WHAT TO LISTEN FOR

Act I: Leonora's aria "Tacea la notte placida . . . Di tale amor." Act II: Azucena's aria "Stride la vampa"; Azucena-Manrico duet "Mal reggendo"; di Luna's aria "Il balen del suo sorriso." Act III: Manrico's aria "Ah, si, ben mio . . . Di Quella pira." Act IV: Leonora's aria "D'amor sull'ali rosee"; Leonora-Manrico-Chorus "Miserere"; Leonora- di Luna duet "Mira, di acerbe lagrime"; Manrico-Azucena duet "Madre, non dormi?"

GIOCOMO PUCCINI

Turandot

Three Acts: First Performance, Milan (La Scala), 1926
Libretto by G. Adami and R. Simoni

WHERE AND WHEN
Peking, legendary times

WHO'S WHO
Turandot, Princess of Peking (soprano)
Calaf, exiled Prince of Tartary (tenor)
Timur, his father (bass)
Liù, slave to Timur and Calaf (soprano)

WHAT IT'S ABOUT
Princess Turandot is the quintessential cruel beauty: "the ice
that gives off fire." The exiled Prince Calaf solves the three
riddles required to win her hand, but he must take far more
dramatic steps to win her heart.

WHAT'S HAPPENING
In Act I, Turandot's most recent suitor is to be executed, having failed to pass the trial-by-riddles. Present for the occasion
is Calaf, who catches sight of the Princess and declares that he
will be the next to try. He gets his chance in Act II, and he
answers all three questions correctly. But Turandot is so dis-
traught at his success that he poses a riddle of his own: if she
can guess his name by morning, he will die as did all the suit-
ors before him. Act III brings a desperate search for Calaf's
name; Turandot has Liù tortured and then watches as the girl
kills herself to protect the secret. Calaf reproaches Turandot
for her heartlessness, but he goes on to embrace her and to
reveal his name. Instead of calling for his execution, she calls
out his name—and it is "Love."

WHAT'S MORE . . .
Turandot, Puccini's last opera (which he died before completing), is, in many ways, the apotheosis of his art. The surreal
rising of the moon in Act I is weirdly impressionistic, the
ensemble that closes the act, beginning with Liù's and Calaf's

arias and ending with the striking of the gong that will change Calaf's fate, is suspenseful enough to please any fan of *verismo*; the commedia dell'arte trio of Ping, Pang and Pong in Act II is an ideal comic interlude; and Turandot's music—so strong, yet so lyrical—is the perfect example of what Puccini referred to musically as "striking out on new paths." (As well as the "new," we also see the old Puccini in Liù's music: it could be Mimì's or Manon's.) In with the light tunefulness, we get the acme of darkness he had only hinted at in earlier operas, and the abundance of shadows makes us sad, all the more, for his untimely death.

WHAT TO LISTEN FOR

Act I: Liù's aria "Signore, ascolta"; Calaf's aria "Non piangere, Liù ."
Act II: Turandot's aria "In questa reggia"; Riddle Scene "Straniero, ascolta!"
Act III: Calaf's aria "Nessun dorma"; Liù 's death scene "Tu, che di gel sei cinta."

ALBAN BERG

Wozzeck

Three Acts: First Performance, Berlin
(State Opera), 1925
Libretto by the composer

WHERE AND WHEN
Leipzig, 1824

WHO'S WHO
Franz Wozzeck, a soldier (baritone)
Marie, his common-law wife (soprano)
Drum major (tenor) **Captain** (tenor)
Doctor (bass)
Child (treble)

WHAT IT'S ABOUT

Wozzeck must endure lectures on immorality from his
Captain; worse, he must undergo experiments by the Doctor
for money to support Marie and their illegitimate son. When
he discovers that Marie has been unfaithful, his already tor-
mented mind snaps, and everything ends in a wash of blood.

WHAT'S HAPPENING

In Act I, Wozzeck undergoes his daily trials with the Captain
and the Doctor. Constantly distracted, he fails to give Marie
the attention she craves, and she gives in to the advances of
the Drum Major. Wozzeck discovers her infidelity in Act II.
Suffering from the taunts of the Captain, the Doctor, and the
Drum Major, Wozzeck hallucinates about a knife. In Act III,
Marie repents, but to no avail. Wozzeck takes her into the
woods and cuts her throat. He later returns to the pond where
he threw the knife and then goes into the water himself, going
deeper and deeper until he drowns. Marie and Wozzeck's
child, unable to comprehend the loss of his parents, continues
to play on his hobby horse at the final curtain.

WHAT'S MORE . . .

Ten years elapsed between the time Berg saw the play *Woyzeck*
by George Büchner and the presentation of his opera based on
it, and when it finally did happen it was like a thunderbolt.
Despite the fact that the opera is very formally composed—
there is a fugue, a symphony in five movements, a sonata, a
passacaglia—the atonality of the music and immorality of the
libretto shocked and horrified much of the audience. One
critic called Berg "a Chinaman from Vienna," and said that
the opera was "a deliberate swindle . . . fragments, sobs, belch-
es . . . an ugly-sounding cackle." The reviews were so hysterical that Berg's publisher had them bound in a little volume
and distributed! The next year, a production in Prague started
a riot in which the mayor died of a heart attack, and to this
day, people become excessive when they speak of Berg's music.

WHAT TO LISTEN FOR

Act I: Marie-Margaret-Wozzeck scene "Tschin Bum . . . !"
Act II: Doctor, Captain, Wozzeck scene "Wohin so eilig . . . ?"
Act III: Marie's murder scene "Dort links geht's in die
Stadt"; orchestral interlude before final scene.

WOLFGANG AMADEUS MOZART

Die Zauberflöte
(The Magic Flute)

Two Acts: Vienna, (Theater auf der Weiden), 1791
Libretto by Emanuel Schikaneder

WHERE AND WHEN
Egypt, legendary time

WHO'S WHO
Tamino, an Egyptian prince (tenor)
Queen of the Night (soprano)
Pamina, her daughter (soprano)
Papageno, a birdcatcher (baritone)
Sarastro, High Priest of Isis and Osiris (bass)
Papagena, female birdcatcher (soprano)

WHAT IT'S ABOUT
Traditional fairy tale elements (magical instruments, wicked queen versus noble "wizard," ordeals by fire and water, everything happening by threes) intermingle with symbols important to the Masonic movement, of which both Mozart and Schikaneder were followers. The characters are thinly disguised figures of the times (including the anti-Masonic Empress Maria Theresa as the Queen of the Night), and the theme

celebrates the triumph of courage, virtue, and wisdom—key requisites for the Masonic "brotherhood of man."

WHAT'S HAPPENING

A giant serpent sets the first scene, as Tamino battles for his life. His rescuers are the Three Ladies of the Queen of the Night. They show him a picture of Pamina, the Queen's daughter, who can be his if he will rescue her from the supposedly evil Sarastro. Accompanied by the clownish Papageno, Tamino begins his quest. He finds not only Pamina, but the truth as well: that Sarastro is the force for good, and the Queen—consumed with hate—is really the villain of the piece. In Act II, with Pamina as his guide, Tamino survives his trials, and both become initiates into Sarastro's noble order. Even Papageno triumphs, by ending up with Papagena, the feathered female of his dreams. Not so lucky is the Queen of the Night: she and her dark Ladies are banished by a sudden flood of the purest and noblest light.

WHAT'S MORE . . .

The Magic Flute is so complex a work that what one hears about it is invariably confusing, too often focused on only one aspect. Its music is, for instance, often referred to as "sublime," which has for its synonyms "exalted" and "noble," and this would certainly fit in with the thoughts of George Bernard Shaw, who wrote that the music of Sarastro "would not be out of place in the mouth of God." But so popular are the melodies for Papageno's music that they are practically folksy. Here is an opera that, at one level, is an esoteric allegory of Freemasonry; at another, a fairy tale to be enjoyed by children of all ages. The answer to these seeming contradictions is that they are all true and all are beside the point: "Flute" is great entertainment, filled with characters and situations that are both believable and unbelievable. It was the greatest success of Mozart's lifetime. This is not an opera for anyone in particular; it is for everybody.

TO LISTEN FOR

Act I: Papageno's entrance aria; Tamino's "Bildnis" aria, as he gazes at a portrait of Pamina; the quintet in which Papageno is punished for lying by the Three Ladies. Act II: Sarastro's "In diesen heil'gen Hallen"; the Queen of the Night's vengeance aria "Die Hölle Rache"; Pamina's sad "Ach ich fühls"; Papageno's duet with his Papagena.

ABOUT THE AUTHORS:
Robert Levine writes regularly
on opera for the national press.
He is author of Consumer
Reports' *Guide to Opera & Dance
on Videocassette* and editor of
Tower Records' magazine,
Classical Pulse. Elizabeth Lutyens
is a feature writer and also editor
of *Video Opera House Quarterly.*